THE TIMES OF
SAINT DUNSTAN

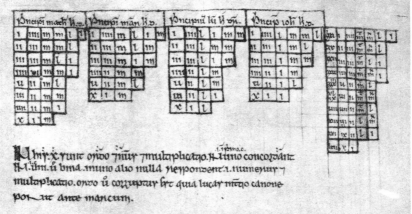

Uñr x̄ runt oñdo ĩuur 7 multaplicatio. ꝯ uno concordãt
ꝯ ĩum. u una. uno alio nulla responden̄a. numeñur 7
multaplicatio. oñdo ũ corruptur sed quia lucar̄ ñico canone
por̄ ut ante mancum.

Incipit alea euangelii quam dubñz epr bañchonsis retulit
apege anglorum to 2 a domni adalradi regir angloum.
despicta a quodam francone 7 a romano gaphice to 2 ĩut.

Qui uol̄ut ꝑitie hanc aleam ꝑsine. illi añ oĩa hr̄ ꝺisciplie vocumēt li uñi ꝑcie
añno necē sit. vuck̄ sꝭcet 7 comite ꝑpugnatorsꝭ 7 impugnatorsꝭ cuutate
seuatailam. 7 regnatour bir.

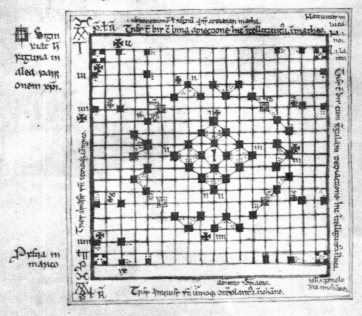

THE TIMES OF
SAINT DUNSTAN

THE FORD LECTURES
delivered in the University of Oxford
in the Michaelmas Term, 1922

J. ARMITAGE ROBINSON

OXFORD
AT THE CLARENDON PRESS

Oxford University Press, Ely House, London W.1

GLASGOW NEW YORK TORONTO MELBOURNE WELLINGTON
CAPE TOWN SALISBURY IBADAN NAIROBI LUSAKA ADDIS ABABA
BOMBAY CALCUTTA MADRAS KARACHI LAHORE DACCA
KUALA LUMPUR SINGAPORE HONG KONG TOKYO

FIRST PUBLISHED 1923
REPRINTED LITHOGRAPHICALLY IN GREAT BRITAIN
AT THE UNIVERSITY PRESS, OXFORD
BY VIVIAN RIDLER
PRINTER TO THE UNIVERSITY
1969

PREFACE

THE main purpose of these Lectures is to trace the origin and progress of the religious movement which is inseparably interwoven with the political history of England in the Tenth Century.

It is men who make movements, however true it be that the movements are only made in a time which is ripe for them. Four men stand out pre-eminent in our period : four distinct personalities, whom we need to know if we would understand the unification of England and the advance which resulted from a renewed contact with the wider civilization across the sea. These are Athelstan, Dunstan, Ethelwold, and Oswald. For each of the last three we have a biography written by a devout admirer, if not an actual disciple, and written within twenty-five years of his death. It is a narrow and even a prejudiced view that they give us : how could it be otherwise where the declared motive is the edification of the reader ? But we can test and supplement these narratives by evidence drawn from various quarters ; and, when we have done so, we feel justified in regarding them as offering an illustration of Bede's generous maxim that kindly judgements make the best history.

For Athelstan, cut off in his greatness before the work of the others was fairly begun, we have unhappily no such aid. Even the fulsome panegyric of a contemporary versifier is known to us only in tantalizing scraps. But Athelstan deserves study. He was the opener of the door : he made much possible that he never lived to see. We must do our best to pick up such fragmentary notices of him as time has spared, and add them to the meagre chronicle of his victories in war.

I have not attempted to tell the general story of the time. I have used the lecturer's privilege of being discursive, and have lingered on topics that interested myself. I have sought to throw out hints for the future historian, and to guard him against many misapprehensions that now pass as true history. These studies are necessarily critical : but I trust that I shall not seem ungrateful to earlier writers whose work has made mine possible.

It will be convenient to mention here some preliminary essays, the results of which are of necessity assumed without further proof in the Lectures.

1. *Some Memories of St Dunstan in Somerset* (Somerset Archaeological and Natural History Society, Proceedings for 1916, vol. LXII, pp. xxvii–xxxvii and 1–25). This is mainly of local interest, dealing with Dunstan's birthplace, 'Dunstan's Dyke', the Bounds of the Twelve Hides of Glastonbury, &c. But it also contains a description of John of Wallingford's Chronicle, with special reference to his account of K. Athelstan and St Dunstan.

2. *The Coronation Order in the Tenth Century* (Journal of Theological Studies, Oct. 1917, xix. 50–72). Incidentally this paper may be found useful for the criticism of the somewhat overestimated Anonymous Life of St Oswald, which calls for further investigation.

3. *The Saxon Bishops of Wells :* a Historical Study in the Tenth Century (British Academy Supplemental Papers, no. IV : Oxford University Press, 1918).

4. *St Oswald and the Church of Worcester* (the same, no. V, 1919).

5. *Somerset Historical Essays* (for the British Academy, Oxford University Press, 1921). The essay on William of Malmesbury's ' De Antiquitate

Glastoniensis Ecclesiae' and that on the Saxon Abbots of Glastonbury deal with topics belonging to our period.

I desire to thank the Delegates of the Clarendon Press for undertaking the publication of these Lectures, and the President and Fellows of Corpus Christi College for allowing the reproduction of the page of their MS, no. 122, which contains the *Alea Evangelii*.

As we review our studies of the Tenth Century, we feel that for England at any rate this was a century of movement, of advance. Yesterday indeed was not better than to-day: but it was different, and some of its differences challenge our attention. The general level of enlightenment and of goodness was not so high: but the heroes of advance stand out in majesty. They were not better, greater souls than we have now in high places. But the big man counted for more: he was bigger relatively than his equal of to-day. He stood out against a darker background: he had more direct responsibility. So he had to take greater risks, and often to suffer for his words and actions. We could wish to know more of these great men: but our records are very scant.

They were men of acts, not of words ; and they left little or nothing in writing. But we know enough to be proud of them as the first makers of our national unity.

J. ARMITAGE ROBINSON.

The Deanery, Wells.
Whitsuntide, 1923.

CONTENTS

CONTENTS

INTRODUCTION

THE ninth century closed with K. Alfred's death. If we are to understand the great religious movement of the tenth century in England, we must begin by recalling Alfred's lament over the gross ignorance of clergy and laity alike which had resulted from the devastation of the houses of religion. It is amazing to find that Wessex could produce no scholars at all. Though we have no evidence that Glastonbury was ever sacked by the Danes, it had shared in the general collapse, doubtless because for a whole generation all men of worth had been fighting for their homes. On the other hand parts of Mercia and of Wales would seem to have been spared, and Worcester in particular had never been quite merged in the prevailing darkness. Alfred found four Mercian scholars to assist him in translating Latin books into the English tongue—Werfrith the bishop of Worcester, and Athelstan a Worcester priest, besides Plegmund and Werwulf who may also have been of the Worcester school. Distant St David's gave him the learned Asser. It is to be noted that not one of these men, so far as we can tell, was a monk; and we have other reason for believing that Worcester had no monks until St Oswald introduced them nearly a century later. Yet Alfred's instinct led him to found two monasteries. One of these, at Shaftesbury, was for women, and his daughter Athelgeofu became its first abbess. The other, at Athelney, was for men; but for this he could find no recruits among the better class of Englishmen, and was obliged to start with foreigners under John the Old Saxon as their abbot, in the hope that they might train up a younger generation: but the experiment was no great success, and for all his care Athelney never rose above mediocrity. He also planned a monastery at Winchester: it was built by his son Edward, and at its head was placed Grimbald, a learned monk of St Bertin's whom Alfred had brought over. But the time for the revival of English monasticism was not yet. Alfred had recognized the need of it, but the foreign plant would not grow on English soil: the movement when it came was of native birth, growing out of the ancient stock, and not an importation from abroad.

Another need of the Church in Wessex was an increase of the episcopate. It was two centuries since the great diocese of Winchester had been divided, and Aldhelm had become the first bishop of Sherborne. It may well be that Alfred contemplated a further subdivision: for the counties of Wilts, Somerset and Devon had now their own aldermen, and it was time that they should have bishops of their own. But, if this was in his mind, he got no further than giving Exeter to Bishop Asser, who was specially qualified to deal with the West Welsh, as they were called, of Devon and Cornwall. Asser, however, presently became bishop of Sherborne, and matters remained as before. It was not until ten years after Alfred's death that a bolder scheme was undertaken by Archbishop Plegmund with the co-operation of K. Edward the Elder. A new diocese was formed out of Winchester, giving a bishop to Wilts with his seat at Ramsbury; and two new dioceses were formed out of Sherborne, giving bishops to Somerset and Devon with their seats at Wells and Crediton. The moment was exceptionally favourable: for Denewulf the bishop of Winchester had died in 908, and Asser the bishop of Sherborne shortly afterwards. Accordingly Plegmund was able to consecrate seven bishops on one memorable day: Frithestan for Winchester; Athelstan, who may well be the Worcester priest whom Alfred had summoned as his helper, for Ramsbury; Wærstan for Sherborne; Athelm, the uncle of St Dunstan and the future archbishop of Canterbury, for Wells; Eadulf for Crediton; as well as Beorneh for the South Saxons and Coenulf for the Mercians at Dorchester. A legend grew up round the unusual event and connected it with a supposed intervention of Pope Formosus of unhappy memory; but the bare facts are beyond contradiction; the only doubt concerns the precise year, and for this the evidence points on the whole to 909 rather than 910.

Edward the Elder was a martial prince, with something of his father's statesmanship, but with no marked interest in learning and religion. The main achievement of his reign was the recovery of those parts of Mercia which had been occupied by the Danes, and their protection for the future

B

by a series of *burhs* or fortresses. In this work he had the powerful co-operation of his sister Ethelfleda, the Lady of the Mercians. Mercia had sought Alfred's aid against the Danes, and had in consequence come under the control of the Wessex kings. Alfred had given his daughter Ethelfleda in marriage to Ethelred the alderman of Mercia, and they ruled together as Lord and Lady of Mercia. London also in 886 had been placed by Alfred under their government ; but when Ethelred died in 911, K. Edward took London and Oxford into his own hand. The warrior Lady still ruled Mercia and carried forward her conquests and fortifications; but on her death in 918 Edward took over the whole of Mercia, setting aside any claim that might have been urged in favour of her daughter. There seems to have been some feeling of discontent at an arrangement by which the last tokens of Mercian independence disappeared.

The Anglo-Saxon Chronicle which owed its origin to Alfred was essentially a Wessex document, but for part of Edward's reign some copies of it have embodied a brief Mercian chronicle, which relates the doings of Ethelred and Ethelfleda and records events of the years 902 to 924. Its dates do not always tally with those of the main Chronicle, but where they are in agreement we can hardly question their accuracy. In the three dates of chief significance the Mercian document agrees with the main Chronicle, when the evidence of the latter is freed from certain complications which have obscured it. The dates in question are the death of Ethelred, 911; the death of Ethelfleda, 918; the death of K. Edward, 924.

The history of the tenth century has been thrown of late into so much confusion by reason of the erroneous dates assigned to some of its leading events, that it is impossible to avoid a certain amount of chronological discussion at the outset of our inquiries. Incidentally this will have the advantage of bringing us face to face with the principal source of our information as to the general framework of the history, namely the various forms in which the Anglo-Saxon Chronicle has been preserved to us. All students of the period owe a debt of gratitude to Mr Plummer's learned edition, which is indeed quite indispensable. But the more delicate problems of chronology require a constant recourse to the original manuscripts, and the history of the various recensions can never be fully worked out until it is possible to examine them side by side with the aid of photographic reproductions. It is hardly possible to conceive a greater service to the study of early English history than would be rendered by the issue of a facsimile edition from one of our University Presses.

In what follows I must ask the benevolent forbearance alike of those who are familiar with the Chronicle and its problems, and of those who have no special acquaintance with the subject. To the former I shall be repeating much that is quite elementary, and occasionally they may think me dogmatic and mistaken in my judgements; to the latter I may find it difficult to make myself intelligible owing to my desire for brevity of statement, but I can assure them that it will be my own fault if the subject proves unprofitable or dull.

Our earliest and most valuable manuscript, that which is known by the symbol A, was given by Archbishop Parker to Corpus Christi College in Cambridge. It is written by one scribe from the beginning down to the year 891 [1]: after this it is carried on by various scribes apparently at Winchester. The seventh of these scribes ends with what he has numbered as the year 923. Half a page is left blank after this. No. 8 will begin a new reign on a new page, and indeed on the first page of a new gathering: for the manuscript was laid aside and neglected for a full generation, and we shall find that the scribe (No. 8) who took it up again about the year 955 could find very little to record for the earlier part of the intervening years. This period of neglect is sadly to be lamented; for the consequence is that the Chronicle almost entirely fails us, where we should specially have valued its full and contemporaneous evidence, in the splendid years of K. Athelstan's reign.

The Parker Chronicle (A) was carried on again after 958 by a succession of hands, still as it would seem at Winchester, until the year 1001. Then again it was laid aside, and this time for about seventy years. Then we find that it has come to Canterbury, where three or four hands work upon

[1] Ending with the arrival of the Scots from Ireland, followed by the year-number 892.

it; but it has only ten entries for the whole period from 1002 to 1070. At some year between these two dates, perhaps about 1025, a copy was made of it. This perished, all but a few fragments, in the fire which consumed so many of the Cotton MSS in 1731; but Wheloc had used it for his edition in 1643; and, yet earlier, William Lambard had made a somewhat abbreviated transcript of it in 1564, which is preserved at Trinity College, Dublin.

Such in outline is the story of the Parker Chronicle, so far as it is necessary to tell it here. We shall be chiefly concerned with alterations which have been made in it, and with glosses inserted by its later owners at Canterbury. One change made long ago has not ceased to be mischievous even to-day. The scribe (No. 8) whom we have spoken of as resuming the Chronicle after the lapse of a generation, and starting afresh on a new gathering of leaves, began his work by entering a series of numerals on successive lines for the years 924 to 932. He could do this safely, because he had nothing to record after 924 (K. Edward's death and Athelstan's accession) until 932. But by an unfortunate piece of carelessness he omitted the number 930 altogether. Now some one at a later day changed 929 into 930, 928 into 929, and so forth, all the way back to 892 which is changed into 893. We cannot indeed be sure that this corrector's motive was to supply the missing number 930. Perhaps we shall be wiser to think of him as a more serious critic who had another copy of the Chronicle before him, such as C, which in fact gives A's annal of 892 under 893, and continues for some time to be a year in advance of A. But whatever the motive the mischief was done, and all the numbers in A from 892 to 929 have been altered by the addition of a year. As to the date of the alteration we can say with certainty that it was before the burnt Cotton MS was written *c.* 1025; for Wheloc's edition gives the altered numbers, and Lambard's transcript bears him out. I am myself quite convinced that the original figures give us on the whole the right dates, and that the alteration ought never to have been made. It is most unfortunate that the latest editors, Mr Thorpe and Mr Plummer, have printed the altered dates for all these years, so that the reading of A is constantly misquoted by historians.

I owe so much to Mr Plummer that I should wish at once to add that of course the editors are entitled to print as their text the dates which they believe to be true, warning us as they do in their footnotes of the original reading of the manuscript; but as most students go to the Chronicle for the events of a particular year, and seldom read it consecutively, it would have saved much misunderstanding if the original year had always been inserted in brackets.

I pass on to speak of the recensions of the Chronicle designated B and C. B (*Tiberius* A 6) was written about the year 1000; it stops at 977. C (*Tib.* B I) was written by various hands between fifty and sixty years later; its annals as far as 977 come from the same copy as B: that copy was then at Abingdon, and at Abingdon C was continued down to 1066. When the original of B and C had been written as far as the year 915, there came to hand the Mercian chronicle, of which we have spoken above, containing events of the years 902 to 924. As it was too late to work in its earlier years with what had been already written, the scribe simply copied it *en bloc* after his annal of 915. Where the manuscript was at this time we cannot tell. We know by the entry of 977 that it was at Abingdon in that year.[1] Abingdon had been revived under St Ethelwold by that time, and we can understand that copies of the Chronicle should be made by the monks of the new house. But in the first quarter of the century Abingdon was a derelict monastery, whose estates had been taken over by K. Alfred, with the exception of a small portion left to support a few clerks. We should more naturally look to Worcester, where learning would seem never to have wholly died out.

Another recension which has made use of the Mercian chronicle is D (*Tib.* B 4), commonly called the Worcester Chronicle. It was written about 1100: its last annal is 1079. We shall speak presently of its earlier history, which is linked up with that of E. Here we would only note that instead of inserting the Mercian annals of 902 to 924 *en bloc* after the year 915 (as in B and C), it makes an attempt to work them in with the other available materials. This it does very clumsily, omitting some annals and misplacing others, and

---

[1] Probably earlier, in 971.

sometimes giving the same event in different words under separate years.

E is the Peterborough Chronicle (Bodl. *Laud. Misc.* 636), given to Oxford by Archbishop Laud. It is written by various hands from 1121 to 1154. As far as 890 it differs little from D, save for some entries in Latin and some insertions relating to Peterborough. In this early part D and E have some distinctive features in common: for they insert a number of passages from Bede's Ecclesiastical History, and they make use of a series of Northumbrian annals between 733 and 806. This suggests that a copy of the Chronicle in its earliest form went to a northern monastery, such as Ripon, where it was written out with modifications and additions. Of this modified recension one descendant presently travelled south and received the Mercian annals, and in course of time produced D: while another copy came after 1022 to St Augustine's, Canterbury, was carried on by the monks there, and was copied a hundred years later as the basis of the Peterborough Chronicle (E).

We come, last of all, to F (*Domit.* A 8). This was written by a Canterbury scribe at the end of the eleventh century. Living in the days of Lanfranc and Anselm, he wished to make the Chronicle intelligible to the Normans, and so he followed up the Saxon entries with a Latin translation. He epitomized a good deal, lest his book should become too bulky. He based his work mainly on the manuscript which was afterwards copied to make the Peterborough Chronicle

(E). Assuming that he was a Christ Church monk, we must suppose him to have borrowed that manuscript from St Augustine's. But he had A in his own house, and he often made use of it. He was struck by the extraordinary neglect of Canterbury history in this manuscript, which had come from Winchester. It was monstrous, for example, that Dunstan's name did not once occur in it. Neither his birth nor his appointment to Glastonbury Abbey, his banishment nor his appointment to Worcester and to London, his accession to Canterbury nor his death, found any record. These omissions the writer of F supplied, as well as many others, in his own new Chronicle: and not content with this he actually wrote most of them into A, as the evidence of the handwriting proves: there is even reason to believe that he made some interpolations into the MS which he had borrowed from St Augustine's. A school of history was growing up at Christ Church, Canterbury, represented by Osbern the precentor and a little later by the more famous Eadmer, the pupil and biographer of St Anselm. To this school the compiler of F must have belonged. I should be willing to believe that he was that very Osbern who achieved a sinister fame by rewriting the Life of St Dunstan.

I have thought it necessary to state at the outset my position in regard to the various recensions of the Chronicle, so as to clear the way for future reference to it. Nothing is more tantalizing than to find the Chronicle quoted as if it were a single definite authority, and nothing

is more misleading than to be told that the Parker
Chronicle places an event under a certain year,
when in fact the original form of the manuscript
assigned it to the year before. Then again, the
scribe of F was not the only Canterbury monk
who made interpolations in the Parker Chronicle;
and all these Canterbury entries represent post-
Conquest opinions and must be judged accordingly. Some of them are no doubt correct, and
were taken from trustworthy sources; others are
quite certainly wrong, and have served to make
bad history.

II

K. ATHELSTAN: HIS ACCESSION AND FIRST YEARS

I<small>F</small> we are to understand the early life of St Dunstan, we must first learn something of K. Athelstan, at whose court he found himself immediately after the death of his uncle Athelm, the archbishop of Canterbury. The Chronicle, which gives us vivid narratives of the times of Alfred and Edward the Elder, suddenly fails us with the accession of Athelstan. A study of the hands which wrote the Parker Chronicle (A) shows that the manuscript was laid aside towards the end of K. Edward's reign and not taken up again for more than a generation. The impulse which K. Alfred had given to the record of contemporary history had lasted for some twenty years after his time. Though we have no reason to connect the writing of the Chronicle with Archbishop Plegmund, it is nevertheless a significant fact that his death occurred in 923, and with him the last of Alfred's scholarly ecclesiastics passed away. Be the cause what it may, this failure of the Chronicle is tantalizing in the extreme. Apart from his accession and his death only two events of general interest are recorded for K. Athelstan's reign— the expedition into Scotland told in a couple of lines, and the battle of Brunanburh as narrated in the famous ballad: the scribe has eked out this scanty history with the insertion of the accessions and deaths of the bishops of Winchester. Of the other recensions D alone gives us further help, telling us of Northumbrian events for two of the earlier years of the reign.

Accordingly when William of Malmesbury was writing his *Gesta Regum* in 1125, he found himself in difficulties for lack of trustworthy material. He had a recension of the Chronicle which for this reign corresponded with our D; and besides this nothing but a forged Malmesbury charter and a few legendary tales, mainly it would seem in ballad form and in his judgement far from trustworthy. However, after he had begun to write with this slender outfit, he happily came across a narrative poem in the Latin language. He describes it as replete with adulation of the king; but he gathered from it some valuable facts as to Athelstan's conflicts with the Northumbrians and the Scots, and also with the Britons both of Wales and of Devon and Cornwall. It also provided him with an account of the marriages of Athelstan's sisters to foreign princes, and of an embassy sent by Hugh the Great, wrongly entitled King of the Franks, to negotiate for the hand of one of these ladies. Traces of the exaggerated language of the poem, and even some tags from it, are to be discovered in his narrative, and he also gives two substantial quotations which show us of what poor stuff it was made. From the forged charter he tells the story of the drowning of Athelstan's brother Edwin, which he is

however unwilling to believe; and from a ballad
or legend a romantic account of Athelstan's birth.
But he is fully conscious that the materials at his
disposal fall far short of the greatness of the
subject: for he says more than once that the
glories of Athelstan threw all his predecessors
into the shade. He was no doubt the more
favourably inclined towards him for his bene-
factions to the abbey of Malmesbury, where his
body lay.

But we must return to the Chronicle and deal
with the obscure question of the date of Athelstan's accession. I should wish at this point to
pay a tribute to a young historical student
whose early death we have reason to lament.
Mr Murray L. Beaven made his mark by three
essays in the *English Historical Review* for the
years 1917 and 1918. The first of them was on
the regnal years of Alfred, Edward the Elder,
and Athelstan. The death of Alfred he placed
in October 899; and he subsequently showed that
the Chronicle of the Alfredian period reckoned the
year as beginning with the Indiction in September.
This explains the entry of Alfred's death by the
original hand in A under the year 900; for that
year was considered to have begun on 24 September 899. The death of Edward the Elder he
placed in 925, and the death of Athelstan in
October 939. In regard to the latter event I think
that he was right, though no modern historian
had put it before 940. In regard to the former
I am sure that he was wrong, and I shall have to
give my reasons for so saying. But I recognize

that he made a fair case for his view, and I regard
these three essays of his as a remarkable contribution to the history of the tenth century.

We come then to consider the evidence for the
date of K. Edward's death and the accession of
K. Athelstan, beginning with the entries in the
various MSS of the Chronicle. The original entry
in A ran thus:

924. Here King Edward died, and Athelstan his son
came to the throne.

At some time before 1025 the year was changed
into 925. Then after the Conquest two Canterbury
hands made new entries. The first wrote: ',and
St Dunstan was born'; the second, who was the
scribe of F, added: 'and Wulfelm came to the
archbishopric at Canterbury'. These two additions, both of them wrong, will have to be noticed
later.

What concerns us here is that the scribe (No. 8)
of A, writing about the year 955, and starting his
work on the first leaf of a new gathering, though
half a page was left vacant by his predecessor,
places Edward's death and Athelstan's accession
in 924, and has no more to say about them.

The Mercian chronicle, represented by B and C,
is much more interesting :

924. Here King Edward died in Mercia at Fearndune;
and Ælfwerd his son very soon after this died at Oxford;
and their bodies lie at Winchester. And Athelstan was
chosen to be king by the Mercians, and hallowed at
Kingston. And he gave his sister . . .

At this point the Mercian chronicle breaks off

altogether with an unfinished sentence. We note, first of all, that here also K. Edward's death is assigned to 924, as by the original scribe in A. Next we observe the importance attached by the Mercian chronicler to the election of Athelstan by the Mercians; and we may mention in this connexion that William of Malmesbury informs us, probably on the authority of his Latin poem, that Athelstan had as a youth been trained at the court of Ethelred and Ethelfleda, the Lord and Lady of Mercia—a stroke of policy on K. Edward's part, which now bore good fruit. Kingston is on the Surrey bank of the Thames, but it bordered on territory which had been ruled by Ethelred, the Mercian alderman, until K. Edward took it over at his death in 911. It was therefore a fit place for the coronation of a king who was chosen by both peoples.

We pass on to the entry of D. This is the same as in B and C, and under the same year 924. But there are two additions: (1) 'about sixteen days' is awkwardly inserted after the words 'Ælfweard his son very soon after this died' and before the words 'at Oxford'; (2) the broken -sentence 'and he gave his sister' is completed by the addition 'over sea to the son of the king of the Old Saxons'. This is no more than a bad guess; for Edith was not married to the Saxon Otto until 929. We can find the true supplement to the broken sentence, if we read D's next annal, and if we take into account its writer's habit of duplicating events which he has found in different sources under different dates. From some North-

umbrian source he has taken over the following
annal for 925:

Here King Athelstan and Sihtric king of the Northumbrians met at Tamworth, on 3 Kal. Febr.; and Athelstan
gave him his sister.

It seems fairly obvious that one and the same
sister is referred to in the incomplete Mercian
annal of 924 and in the Northumbrian annal of
925. By his unfortunate patchwork D has made
one sister into two, and so carelessly that he has
neither distinguished them by name, nor even by
saying in the second place 'another of his sisters'.
When we understand D's method of work, we
shall not be tempted into thinking, as some have
thought, that he had before him a fuller manuscript of the Mercian chronicle.

Next we will read the annal in F:

925. Here King Edward died, and Athelstan his son
came to the throne; and Wulfelm was hallowed to archbishop of Canterbury, and St Dunstan was born.

The first clause is taken from A's annal of 924,
which before this time had been altered to 925.
As evidence of date, therefore, it is of no value
at all.

I have kept E to the last, for reasons which will
be plain when we look at it. It has, first, under
924, the original entry of A:

924. Here King Edward died, and Athelstan his son
came to the throne.

Then it goes on:

925. Here Bishop Wulfelm was hallowed, and in the
same year King Edward died.

This is plainly a Canterbury correction, which may have been made in the margin of the manuscript from which this Peterborough Chronicle (E) was copied. It has got into E's text, and then some one, observing that it contradicts the annal for 924, has crossed that earlier annal out. Once again, therefore, we see that the date 925 has no authority beyond that of the scribe who at some time before 1025 added a year to the series of dates in A. In short, the Anglo-Saxon Chronicle offers no evidence for any other date than 924 for the death of Edward the Elder and the accession of his son Athelstan.

Why then does Mr Beaven conclude, as we have said, that 925 was the year of K. Edward's death? In the first place he observes that the Chronicle states, *s.a.* 940, that Athelstan reigned 14 years and 10 weeks.[1] If we deduct this period from 27 October 939, which he has shown to be the true date of his death, we get back to the summer of 925 (more exactly to 18 August 925). Next he notes that a charter of St Augustine's, Canterbury, was granted on Athelstan's coronation day, 4 September 925—the date being supported by the fact that this was a Sunday. He thinks it highly improbable that the coronation would have been so long deferred, if K. Edward had died in 924. He has not observed that K. Edward himself was not crowned till Whitsunday, though his father had died in the preceding October.

Then he calls attention to a regnal table contained on a leaf of *Tib.* A 3, which appears once to

---

[1] *Eng. Hist. Rev.*, October 1917, pp. 522 ff.

have formed part of the genealogical preface of the Chronicle B. The periods here ascribed to various reigns are slightly shorter than the corresponding periods in the Chronicle, and, as in four cases out of five they bring us back to Sundays, they are clearly calculated from the date of coronation. Here Athelstan is given 14 years 7 weeks and 3 days, which brings us back to 5 September 925 and a Monday; but the error of a single day he thinks has arisen through 'calculating from a day which was held to begin at Vespers of the previous evening'.

Now the Hyde Register (or *Liber Vitae*) places the death of K. Edward the Elder, whom it regards as the founder of the New Minster, on 17 July, but it does not mention the year.[1] Mr. Beaven holds that K. Edward died on 17 July 925, and that Athelstan's accession took place a month later, when he had buried his father and his brother Ælfwerd at Winchester: his coronation at Kingston followed on 4 September of the same year. Accordingly he believes that the Mercian chronicle (B, C, and D) has dated its annal of 924 a year too soon. He would date it 925, and so bring it into harmony (as he supposes) with the Parker Chronicle (A). But we have been at pains to show that A as originally written had 924.

Now the outstanding facts are these: (1) that

---

[1] This is confirmed by the fragment of an English Calendar of the beginning of the twelfth century, which came from St Évroul (Paris, B. N. lat. 10062 : Delisle, *Extrait du Journal des Savants*, August 1903, p. 10), where we find on 17 July: 'Obitus Eadweardi regis.'

Athelstan was crowned on 4 September 925;
(2) that the Chronicle, including the Mercian
chronicle, places Edward the Elder's death in 924;
(3) that the Mercian annal for 924 gives a series
of events under this one year—Edward's death,
his son Ælfwerd's death, their burial at Winchester, Athelstan's election by the Mercians, his
coronation at Kingston, and his giving his sister
in marriage: we must assume therefore either
that an earlier coronation took place (which is not
likely), or that the annalist has brought the
events of two or even three years into one.

Further we have had occasion to note that the
periods assigned by different authorities to Athelstan's reign suggest that some reckoned it from
18 August 925, and others from 4 September 925,
the coronation day.

Is there any other source to which we may turn
for light on the matter? When Mr Napier and
Mr Stevenson produced their valuable edition of
the Crawford Charters, they gave us as No. IV a
new charter of K. Athelstan, which they regarded
as an undoubted original.[1] This charter is dated
29 April 930 in the sixth year of the reign. This
implies that K. Athelstan was on the throne at
least as early as 29 April 925. It directly contradicts the view that K. Edward did not die
until 17 July 925. Nor does this charter stand
alone: other charters similarly show that he was
reigning on 28 May 925,[2] and almost certainly on

[1] *Anecdota Oxoniensia*, Crawford Charters (1895), p. 5:
cf. Birch, *Cartularium Saxonicum*, 1343.

[2] B. C. S. 702.

23 March in that year; [1] while there is fairly good evidence that he was reigning on 24 December 924.[2] Record evidence such as this cannot be set aside.

It will be seen therefore that, gladly as I welcome other results to which Mr Beaven's careful investigations have led him, I cannot agree with him on this one point. I have thought it right, out of respect to his memory, to give my reasons at some length. But the discussion is by no means fruitless; for several points of interest arise out of it.

For example, though the charters from 930 onwards reckon the regnal year from a date early in 925, if not towards the end of 924, yet there are two exceptional instances, in 928 and 930, which reckon from a later date. The charters are known to us only from copies in chartularies, so that their evidence could not override the evidence of actual charters which still exist; but they seem to bear out the conclusion that we drew from the different periods assigned to K. Athelstan's reign, namely, that some people reckoned from one date and some from another.

First, there is the charter granted at Exeter on Easter Wednesday, 16 April 928.[3] This is said to be in the third year of the reign. It implies that 16 April 926 was in the first year: this 'first year' accordingly could not have begun earlier than 17 April 925; it may have been reckoned from the coronation day, 4 September 925. It is

[1] B. C. S. 674.   [2] B. C. S. 691, 692.
[3] B. C. S. 663; cf. 664.

worth observing that the date is given in a very strange form: 'anno dominicae incarnationis DCCCCXXVIII, mei haut dubium regiminis tercio'. Does the insertion of 'there is no doubt' suggest a date in 925 at which Athelstan's claim was put beyond all question, either the Easter court or the September coronation?

The other charter is a grant to a certain Abbot Cynath.[1] The year is 930, in the third indiction; and it is said to be the fifth year of Athelstan's reign over the Anglo-Saxons and the third of his reign over the Northumbrians and Cumbrians. This would hold for a reign commencing for the Anglo-Saxons at Easter or in September 925, and for the Northumbrians in 927. Now in E of the Chronicle we read under 927 that Athelstan drove out Guthfrith. In D we are told under 926 that Athelstan succeeded to the kingdom of the Northumbrians, but there are some grounds for thinking that this annal should be dated 927. The charter comes from a source which is often untrustworthy: but it is hard to think it the invention of a forger. It has points which link it with the Exeter charter, as for example the curious phrase 'triquadri orbis'.[2]

These exceptional calculations may well suggest that Athelstan's entry upon his father's dominions was not achieved easily or all at once. There may be truth in the legend that he was of illegitimate birth. By the Mercians he is elected first of all, and probably without demur in 924. Then

[1] B.C.S. 667.
[2] For this phrase see below, p. 58.

by Easter in the next year he is more widely recognized, and he is crowned on 4 September. Two years later he gains back the Northumbrian kingdom. After 930 these gradual accessions are no more taken into account, and the reign is calculated from its earliest point.

I shall now ask leave to ramble a little in pursuit of this Abbot Cynath, to whom the charter last mentioned (B. C. S. 667) was granted. In 930 the king gives Dumbleton in Gloucestershire to Cynath, who is picturesquely described as 'archimandrite of monastic conversation', though afterwards he is called plain 'abbot'. He evidently presided over a house of monks. The charter comes to us from the Abingdon History, and there he is said to have been abbot of Abingdon, and to have been succeeded by Godescale, who in turn was succeeded by the reforming abbot St Ethelwold. There is no evidence that Godescale, who bears a German name very uncommon in England, was an abbot at all: he appears in charters as 'sacerdos' and as 'presbyter', and his presence at Abingdon may well be an illustration of K. Athelstan's close relations with the Continent.[1]   Again, there is no evidence that there were monks at Abingdon at this time: the old monastery had been destroyed by the Danes, K. Alfred had taken over the properties, leaving but 40 hides to support the clerks of a small church; and a royal palace would seem to have been built there.

Moreover when we look at the charter we find

[1] So Mr Stenton in his *Early History of Abingdon*, p. 38.

nothing about Abingdon, and we observe that Abbot Cynath gets the estate at Dumbleton as a personal gift with power to dispose of it to his heirs. Indeed we are informed by a confirmatory supplement of K. Edgar's that Abbot Cynath gave it to Bishop Osulf, who was bishop of Ramsbury in Wilts (950–970). It was not until a generation later still that the property came to the newly founded monastery at Abingdon. And the way of it was this. Two and a half manses at Abingdon had come into K. Ethelred's hands through forfeiture from one Athelsige, who stole the swine of Athelwin son of the alderman Ethelmar. The king gave them to Hawas his man, who exchanged them with Wulfric the thegn.[1] Now Wulfric Spot, as he was called, founded the abbey of Burton-on-Trent; and to get confirmation of his will he had to give many presents,[2] and amongst others the vill of Dumbleton was given to Ælfric archbishop of Canterbury. A charter of K. Ethelred then confirmed the whole property of 24 manses (for there had been another forfeiture) to Archbishop Ælfric for a price, and the archbishop finally bequeathed it to Abingdon, where he had been a monk.[3]

As there is nothing further to suggest any connexion between Abbot Cynath and Abingdon, we cannot doubt that the Abingdon historian of the twelfth century, finding this early Dumbleton charter among the muniments, as one of the title

[1] *Hist. Abingd.* i. 390; Kemble, *Cod. Diplom.* 692.
[2] *Hist. Abingd.* i. 411.
[3] K. C. D. 716, 1295, 1298.

deeds of the property, adopted Abbot Cynath as an early abbot of Abingdon, and explained that when Archbishop Ælfric gave Dumbleton to the monks he was only giving back an ancient property which had been fraudulently taken away.

We are free now to pursue Abbot Cynath without any prejudice so far as Abingdon is concerned. His name is not a common one, but we find it in the lists of the Worcester *familia* in the time of K. Alfred's learned helper Bishop Werfrith. Cynath appears in 899, the year of K. Alfred's death, in a list where the first signature after the bishop is 'Cynelm abbas et diaconus'.[1] Then in 904 we find 'Cynath diaconus', and at the head 'Cynehelm abbas'.[2] This Abbot Cynelm interests us, because Worcester had no monks at that time. When we trace him back we find him as a member of the Worcester *familia* in 889;[3] and again in 897, where he is 'Cynelm diaconus'.[4] It would appear from a charter, which is curiously corrupt, but cannot be a mere invention, that in 907 Bishop Werfrith granted to his kinsman Abbot Cynelm Bengeworth, close to Evesham.[5] Before this in 903, Abbot Cynelm attests the interesting Mercian charter by which Duke Ethelfrith gets the renewal of a charter which had perished.[6]

After Abbot Cynelm has disappeared we begin to meet with Cynath as an abbot. Unfortunately we have no lists of the Worcester *familia* after

---

[1] B. C. S. 580; cf. 560.   [2] B. C. S. 608, 609.
[3] B. C. S. 559.   [4] B. C. S. 575.
[5] B. C. S. 616.   [6] B. C. S. 603.

904 for more than fifty years; so that we cannot see whether Abbot Cynath headed the list after Abbot Cynelm had disappeared. But we find that he attests a Mercian grant to Eadric of about 916.[1] Then in 925 he attests K. Athelstan's charter on his coronation day ('Cened abbas'; but most of the names are corrupted).[2] In the same year he is present at a great Mercian assembly, of which more must be said presently. In 929 Coenwald, the bishop of Worcester, himself a monk,[3] took K. Athelstan's gifts to the German monasteries; and it is interesting to find amongst the entries in the St Gall confraternity book on the occasion of this visit the name of 'Kenod abbas'.[4] It is not unlikely that Abbot Cynath accompanied his bishop on this occasion, and that the king's grant of Dumbleton to him in the next year may have been made in recognition of his services.

Bearing in mind that Abbot Cynelm was given Bengeworth, close to Evesham, and that Abbot Cynath received Dumbleton in Gloucestershire which is only some seven miles south of the same place, we turn to the History of the abbey of Evesham. Here we learn from a twelfth-century source that Bengeworth was one of the properties given to St Egwin the founder by K. Coenred of Mercia in 708, but lost with many other estates when (as it was said) the monks were driven out and canons were introduced under K. Edmund:

---

[1] B. C. S. 632.
[2] B. C. S. 641: cf. *The Saxon Bishops of Wells*, pp. 31 f.
[3] See B. C. S. 883, 909, 911, 937; and Flor. Wig., *s. a.* 957.
[4] *The Saxon Bishops of Wells*, p. 61.

it was not recovered till the days of K. Cnut.[1] This is perhaps very doubtful history; but we may safely conclude that by K. Edmund's day here, as in many other places, monasticism had died out, and the abbey had come into lay hands, the church being served by a few clerks until the time of the great reform. The early history of Evesham was for the most part a blank: for the abbots from St Egwin down to Abbot Edwin in K. Edmund's reign we have only a bare list of eighteen names. The last five are given thus:[2]

14. Kinelm.
15. Kinath.
16. Ebba.
17. Kinath II.
18. Edwin.

The entry of two Kinaths may be a mere confusion. But here we have our two abbots, Cynelm and Cynath, one after the other, and our curious little problem has found its solution. Abbot Cynath had been trained at Worcester under the scholarly Bishop Werfrith, and in course of time he had succeeded Abbot Cynelm at Evesham.

In order to find a sure way of approach to the problems of the religious movement of reform in the tenth century, we began by reminding ourselves of K. Alfred's lament over the ignorance of clergy and laity alike, his attempt at a revival of monasticism, his failure to find recruits among

---

[1] *Hist. Evesh.* 72, 84.   [2] *Ibid.*, p. 77.

the English folk, and his introduction of foreign teachers. We noted that, though Wessex was in thick darkness, Wales and Mercia gave him some men of learning, and that Worcester in particular had kept the torch of knowledge alight. Alfred himself laid sure foundations: in his Laws he began with the Decalogue: he learned to read and translate Latin books, and the example thus set must have been in itself impressive: moreover the first books in the English tongue spoke of God and Christ and the Church.

We can but grieve that we know so little of what followed. His learned archbishop, Plegmund, survived him by more than twenty years. A division of dioceses and a consequent increase in the number of bishops, which Alfred had doubtless contemplated, was carried out ten years after his death. His martial son Edward shows statesmanship, but not learning: the wordy charters ascribed to him are late forgeries, and we cannot trust their account of his gifts to pious foundations, though it is plain that he carried out his father's design for a new monastery at Winchester.

The first quarter of the tenth century still leaves our darkness unrelieved. Then comes the flashing brilliance of Athelstan. Plegmund did not live to crown him, having given place to Athelm, who had been the first bishop of the new see of Wells. If we linger on Athelm's almost forgotten name, it is because he was educated at Glastonbury, and so reminds us that the tradition of learning was not wholly broken in that ancient house; and yet more because he was the uncle of Dunstan, whom at the close of his brief primacy he commended to the new king Athelstan.

Athelstan's reign covers but fifteen years. To the chagrin of the historian the Chronicle suddenly ceases to be written; and when it is taken in hand again after some thirty years, only a few leading incidents of the intervening period are entered, with a poem or two, and the successions of the bishops of Winchester. So we have to piece together isolated facts recorded here and there, deductions drawn from charters, petty yet precious entries on the fly-leaves of manuscripts, and notices of gifts of sacred relics made to, or made by, this royal connoisseur. For the rest we must content ourselves with William of Malmesbury's attempt to make use of a poem now lost and of such legends as were not obviously untrustworthy.

There is a charter of 925, which offers so interesting a glimpse of K. Athelstan's first year that I think it worth while to spend a little time upon it. It comes to us from a register of the abbey of Burton-on-Trent, which now forms part of the Hengwrt collection in the possession of the Wynnes of Peniarth (B. C. S. 642). It is written in the strangely inflated Latin of the period, which has been so admirably illustrated by the editors of the Crawford Charters; it is sprinkled with Greek words and is often quite ungrammatical. I shall venture to give it you in a fairly literal translation, though I cannot hope to do justice even to its opening sentence: 'Regnante Theo in perpetuum architectorio':

✠ God reigning for ever, the Architect of the universe.

It is known to be worth while that the blandishments of things present and the deceitful prosperity of the world should be counted of no moment [1]; and whosoever in the felicity of this life desires by the grace of God the boon of eternal blessedness, he is duly bound to recall how the egregious preacher and wise 'Trichelaus' [2] says: ' While we are in the body we are absent from the Lord'.

Wherefore I, Athelstan, by indulgence of divine clemency king of the English, and supervisor of the Christian household of the whole region well-nigh in the whirlpools of cataclysms, was investigating the matter of discussed obedience (*ventilatae obedientiae causam*) brought to notice by the careful sagacity of my faithful lieges, how that I should grant to my faithful thegn Eadric seven manses in that place 'at Hwituntune' for perpetual inheritance : which also I have done : for delivering I delivered it to him, that he should have and possess it for perpetual inheritance, with woods, pastures, meadows and fields, and all things rightly thereto belonging; and afterwards, when he goes the way of all, should leave it to whatsoever heir he will, as we have before said, for eternal inheritance.

For this cause therefore have we ordered this book of inheritance to be written anew, because that ancient book of inheritance we had not. But if any one after this shall bring forward that ancient book, or aught else contrary to this our decision, let it be void of effect to all Christian men and avail nought. Let that land aforesaid be free from all worldly tax, save only these three things, military expedition, and construction of fortress and of bridge.

If any man shall choose to keep and augment this our decree, may the Almighty Governor augment for him all good things of the present and the future life: but if any one (which we hope will not be) shall choose to

[1] The charter says 'monument', but doubtless 'moment' was meant.

[2] I can only imagine that this might mean the Tentmaker.

scheme against or infringe this our decree, let him know that he shall render grave account thereof in the day of judgement before the tribunal of the Lord, except he make amends here beforehand with due penance before his death.

This schedule was promulgated with letters inscribed in the first year of the king aforesaid, in the 925th year from the Incarnation of Our Lord Jesus Christ, in the 13th indiction.

✠ I, Athelstan, king, have confirmed and corroborated this my donation by the triumphal trophy of the Holy Cross with my own fingers.

✠ I, Ælfwine, by the grace of God bishop.

✠ I, Winsige, bishop.

✠ I, Wilfred, bishop, have consented and subscribed.

✠ I, Edgar, bishop, have consented and subscribed.

✠ I, Cynaht, abbot, have consented and subscribed. And the rest, dukes, presbyters and monks, and thegns, to the number of 57.

To put all this in few words: K. Athelstan at a formal assembly makes to Eadric the thegn a new grant of Hwituntune, because the old 'book of inheritance' was lost. The date is 925, in the thirteenth indiction, which ended on 23 September 925: and it is in the first year of the reign.

Our first question is, Where is Hwituntune? We can hardly be wrong in identifying it with Whittington, which lies between Lichfield and Tamworth, and is some twelve miles from Burton-on-Trent, to which the register which has preserved this charter belongs. The locality accords with the attestation of the charter. Four bishops are named and one abbot: all are Mercian or closely connected with Mercia. Lichfield, Dorchester, Worcester, and Hereford are the bishops; and the one abbot is our abbot Cynath of Evesham. Unfortunately the attestation is cut short, after the manner of this register. We have no more names, but the assembly was a great one; for the dukes, presbyters, monks, and thegns numbered fifty-seven. Where our historical information is so slender, we may be grateful for the definite fact that at some time in 925 Athelstan held this great Mercian assembly, without the attendance of the West Saxon bishops. We may well set it side by side with the statement that Athelstan 'was chosen to be king by the Mercians'. Is it even possible that it was at this very assembly that his claims were accepted, and that this is what is referred to in the strange reference to the 'matter of discussed obedience (*ventilatae obedientiae causam*)'?

It is of some interest to trace the story of Eadric the thegn, to whose loss of a charter we owe this important document; for it will introduce us to some of the great people of the time. There are very few charters of Edward the Elder that can be implicitly trusted; but there is one in the British Museum [1] which is accepted as an original. It is of the year 903, and is attested by 'Eadric minister'. It tells us that Duke Ethelfrith had lost all his charters by fire, and that K. Edward, Duke Ethelred, and his wife Ethelfleda, the Lady of the Mercians, renewed to him the charter of Princes Risborough, co. Bucks. There is a similar charter which is preserved only in a corrupt form in Glastonbury chartularies.[2] It is a renewal in the same terms of Duke Ethelfrith's lost charter

[1] Stowe XXI: B.C.S. 603.   [2] B.C.S. 606.

of Wrington in Somerset. This property came afterwards to Glastonbury by gift of the famous Duke Athelstan, the 'Half-king' as he was called, who became a monk of the abbey at the close of his life. And the charter proves, what the editors of the Crawford Charters [1] had ingeniously conjectured, that Duke Athelstan was Duke Ethelfrith's son. For though the note appended to the charter as we have it calls him 'filius Etheredi', there is an ancient list of Glastonbury charters printed by Hearne from a MS at Trinity College, Cambridge, which gives the father's name as Æthelfrithus.[2] The signatures to the Wrington charter are not preserved; otherwise we should probably have found 'Eadric minister' again.

The next incident in Eadric's story takes us on to very slippery ground. It comes in a charter which bears an impossible date, and reaches us from an untrustworthy source, the History of the abbey of Abingdon.[3] Yet we may be disposed to look favourably upon it, as it has the attestation of our abbot Cynath. It is a grant from the Lady Ethelfleda, who is described as 'gubernacula regens Merciorum': it is attested by the bishops of Lichfield, Worcester, and Hereford, and by a bishop Ælfred whose see is uncertain. Duke Ethelfrith attests : also three abbots, Ethelhun, Ecgbert, and Cynath, of whom the first would seem to be the abbot of Berkeley, who makes

---

[1] p. 83.

[2] *John of Glaston.*, p. 371 'Edwardus de Wring. dat Æthelfritho, quam ejus filius Ethelstanus dux ded. G.'

[3] i. 44: B. C. S. 632.

a composition with Duke Ethelred in 883.[1] The second is the abbot whose murder is recorded in the Mercian chronicle under 916. A further coincidence with the Mercian chronicle is that this charter was granted at Weardburg and that in 915 Ethelfleda built a fortress at Weardbyrig.[2] Mr Plummer indeed thinks these coincidences so great as to discredit the charter altogether. But a forger would hardly have been likely to discover the two other Mercian abbots, Cynath and Ethelhun, unless he had made a very systematic search.[3]

In this charter, as afterwards in 925, Eadric the thegn obtains the renewal of a title-deed which had been lost. He had bought the land (Farnborough, co. Berks.[4]) from Wullaf, to whose greatgrandfather Bynna it had been granted by Offa, king of Mercia. ' Now it chanced that the loss of the former book befel in the year of the eclipse of the sun.' The famous eclipse, when people saw

---

[1] B. C. S. 551.

[2] Supposed to be Warburton on the Mersey. 'There is a very rare penny of Athelstan, struck at the mint "Weardbyrig"' (Oman, *England before the Norman Conquest*, p. 501).

[3] Mr Plummer also charges him with making Ethelfleda's daughter sign as a bishop. 'Ælfwyn episcopus' does indeed precede 'Ælfwine episcopus'; but that surely is the error of a copyist, not of a forger.

[4] The same property was granted by K. Athelstan, according to a charter (B. C. S. 682) from which the date is missing, but which seems to belong to 937. It was given (after forfeit from 'Alfric Puer', who had taken it from the widow Eadfled) in K. Ethelred's second charter of restitution (993) to Abingdon (*Hist. Abingd.* i. 368). It was again given to Abingdon by Hardicnut in 1042 (*Ibid.* i. 446).

the stars for half an hour in the afternoon, occurred
on 29 October 878: it is entered in the Chronicle
under 879, as the year was reckoned by the writer
as beginning with the September indiction.

Now the odd thing is that this charter, which
clearly belongs to 915 or 916, is dated 878.
Evidently the year of the eclipse was inserted in
the margin, and through the stupidity of a copyist
has ousted the true date of the charter. No forger
would have given such a date, for it would have
been a plain contradiction of the details which
he had so skilfully brought together. Moreover
a forger would probably have taken the year 879
from the Chronicle, if he had wanted to date the
eclipse: it is more reasonable to suppose that
the charter was in existence at a time when the
actual year of the eclipse was in the memory of
men who did not employ the peculiar reckoning
which the Chronicler employed for the Alfredian
period.

I think we need no longer hesitate to accept this
charter as the corrupt copy of a genuine document
of about the year 915. We go on then to pursue
our inquiry as to Eadric the thegn. Two persons
attest Athelstan's charters of the years 930–32 as
'Eadric minister': after this one attests frequently
until 941. Then from 942 to about 950 we have
the attestation 'Eadric dux'. Let us assume for
the moment that it is our Eadric who survives,
and is made an alderman by K. Edmund in 942.
Then we know that K. Edred grants to 'Eadric
comes' a property at Ashdown in 947 (B. C. S.
828). The property had been given by Duke

Ethelwold in his will 'to my brother Eadric': so that the king's grant was simply a confirmation of this. But here we are on interesting ground: for Duke Ethelwold was the brother of Duke Athelstan, the 'Half-king', who, as we remember, gave to Glastonbury the land at Wrington, for which his father, Duke Ethelfrith, had obtained the renewal of a lost charter in 903.

Duke Eadric then, the brother of Dukes Ethelwold and Athelstan, is the son of that Duke Ethelfrith who lost his charters by fire some time before 903. Are we right in our assumption that Duke Eadric is Eadric the thegn, one or both of whose charters perished in 878 ? It certainly looks as if the same loss of ancestral title-deeds led to these four grants of renewal. It is a small point, but worth noting, that in Duke Ethelfrith's charter of 903 five thegns attest, and the last two are 'Eadric minister' and 'Æthelwold minister'—two of his sons, if our assumption be right. It is of more importance to observe that Duke Ethelfrith's renewals were Mercian charters, granted by K. Edward, Duke Ethelred, and the Lady Ethelfleda; and that Eadric's Farnborough renewal in 915 was granted by the Lady Ethelfleda, when she was sole ruler of Mercia, and his Whittington renewal in 925 was granted by K. Athelstan at a great Mercian assembly probably held at Tamworth. It is difficult not to believe that all the documents were lost in the same fire and in the year of the great eclipse, and that Duke Ethelfrith and Eadric the thegn were father and son.

The importance of our conclusion is not primarily

genealogical. What really matters is that one charter helps to validate another, and we learn once again that suspicious-looking charters from untrustworthy chartularies are often mangled copies of genuine originals, and may yield useful scraps of true history.

III

K. ATHELSTAN: SOME CHARACTERISTIC
INTERESTS

I SHALL not attempt to tell the story of K. Athelstan's wars. That has been done by the vigorous
pen of Sir Charles Oman, and some important
criticisms have since been made by Mr Beaven.
I wish rather to take up points which seem to have
been passed over hitherto, but which help to
characterize the monarch of whom we know so
little. I propose to collect the scattered evidence
which shows him to us first as a donor of manuscripts and secondly as a collector of relics.

A Donor of Manuscripts

We will begin with his gifts to St Cuthbert,
whose body had come from the ruins of Lindisfarne
by a devious route to Chester-le-Street, but had
not yet reached its resting-place at Durham. In
the *Historia Regum,* which goes under the name of
Symeon of Durham,[1] we find appended to a notice

[1] 'Symeon of Durham' is an appellation which has to be
used with caution. The *Historia Regum* consists of two
sharply divided sections, the second of which is introduced
by a Recapitulation of K. Alfred's reign. We are here concerned only with the first section which goes down to the
accession of K. Edgar in 957. It is in itself highly composite:
from 734 to 802 it embodies important Northumbrian annals:
after this it is meagre until Asser's *Life of Alfred* affords
abundant material; when this source fails, it depends mainly

of Athelstan's expedition to Scotland in 934—a notice equivalent to that in A.-S. Chron. E—the statement that the king visited St Cuthbert's shrine and offered many gifts. The writer's language shows that this is only a brief summary of what is to be found elsewhere.[1] In the *Historia Dunelmensis Ecclesiae* we find a like statement,[2] and here we are referred for details to yet another source, a *cartula* cited elsewhere. This we find at last in the *Historia de S. Cuthberto*,[3] where we are told that when Athelstan made an expedition into Scotland he visited St Cuthbert's shrine, and composed a *testamentum* which he placed by the saint's head. A Latin document follows, which on examination proves to be a compilation made from certain English notes of Athelstan's gifts, which had been written into a manuscript which perished in the Cottonian fire of 1731. Of this precious book (*Otho* B 9) only a dozen scraps have survived out of 122 folios. Happily Wanley had described the book in his Catalogue (Hickes's *Thesaurus*, ii. 238), and had copied Athelstan's original dedication. It was a Gospel Book, written as Wanley believed in France; and the entry came before the Gospel of St John. It said: 'I Athelstan king give this book into St Cuthbert,' and it went on to forbid its removal, or the alienation of

on a form of the Chronicle related to the ancestor of E: at a few points it has unique notices of Northern affairs, but their value is not to be estimated by that of the eighth-century Northumbrian annals, with which there is no reason whatever to connect them.

[1] Rolls Ser. edition, ii. 92.
[2] *Ibid.* i. 75.   [3] *Ibid.* i. 211.

his other gifts, on pain of such a fate as that of Judas Iscariot, and of the terrible sentence at doomsday, 'Depart from me ye cursed into everlasting fire.'

This then was one of K. Athelstan's gift books, a copy of the Gospels written somewhere across the Channel. A picture, we are told, was inserted before St Matthew's Gospel, showing the king bending before the saint and offering his book. A note stated that the painting was caused to be done by one 'Benedictus Evernenficus', of whom we could wish to know more.

We must regret that Wanley did not go on to copy the further English entry as to K. Athelstan's other gifts which immediately followed. We have therefore to depend on the Latin record, and from this we need only pick out the books [1]—'one missal, two texts of the Gospels adorned with gold and silver, and one Life of St Cuthbert written in metre and in prose'. It is generally agreed that the last of these books is still preserved in the Library of Corpus Christi College at Cambridge (No. 183). This is a beautiful book, described by Dr M. R. James as written in a fine Anglo-Celtic hand. It contains St Cuthbert's Life in prose and in verse, but it is chiefly famous for its lists of bishops of all the English sees. I have said so much about it elsewhere,[2] that here I will only notice a few points.

Like the Gospel Book it has a picture of a king presenting a book to a saint. It is in the main

[1] See B. C. S. 685.
[2] *The Saxon Bishops of Wells*, pp. 13 f.

a collection of northern materials, but it is a southern copy: for its episcopal successions are brought up to date only for Canterbury and the Wessex dioceses; the others end before *c.* 840. I have suggested Glastonbury as the place of writing.

This book cannot indeed have been given to St Cuthbert in 934; for the bishops of Winchester include Ælfheah the Bald, who did not come in till 934 or 935. On the other hand we note that no successor is given to Ælfheah of Wells, who died in 939 (or 938). From these two facts we may reasonably conclude that the MS was written not later than 939, but was not completed before 935. Yet this is not a decisive argument against the identification. For the year 934 was probably a mere guess of the Durham monk, who saw that date for Athelstan's expedition to Scotland in his copy of the A.-S. Chronicle. The later expedition in 937 would suit us just as well. It is not unlikely that the book was promised in 934, then ordered at Glastonbury, and presented to St Cuthbert in 937.

Interesting evidence of the impression which K. Athelstan made on the monks of St Cuthbert is to be found in their famous *Liber Vitae*, which is now preserved as *Domitian* 7 in the Cottonian Library. The first leaf of this once splendid book was written in letters of gold and silver about the year 840, and contains a list of kings and dukes. There are three columns of twenty names in each: those in the first column are written in gold; those in the second and third columns are written in silver, which unhappily is now represented by blurred and black letters which show through the parchment and generally disfigure the page. The list begins with the great kings Edwin and Oswald. Across the page at the top is the title in red lettering: *Nomina regum vel ducum.* Immediately following it, and in the same line, an early tenth-century hand has written in black ink: ' aedelstan rex'. The scribe has thus given to K. Athelstan the honorific precedence which the splendour of his gifts to St Cuthbert seemed to deserve.

From Northumbria we return south to Canterbury. In the Archbishop's Library at Lambeth there is a small copy of the Latin Gospels, in a fine Irish hand and with exquisite Irish decorations. On f. 3b it has the following inscription:

✠ MÆIELBRIÐVS · MAC
DVRNANI · ISTŸ · TEXTV̄
PER · TRIꝰVADRV̄ · DŌ
DIGNE · DOGMATIZAT
✠ AST · AETHELSTANVS
ANGLOSÆXANA · REX · ET
RECTOR · DORV̆ERNENSI
METROPOLI · DAT · PÆVV̄

This book belongs to a famous group of Irish Gospels, important alike for the character of their text and for their illuminations. It shares with the Book of Kells, St Chad's Gospels, and the Lindisfarne Gospels the notable feature that the genealogy at the beginning of St Matthew is treated as introductory, and the Gospel proper is made to begin at the words *Christi autem generatio* (i. 18), which form the subject of a splendidly illuminated page.[1]   The date of the writing has been much disputed.   It has been assigned by some textual critics to the early part of the tenth century, on the ground that it was written by Maelbrighde Mac Durnan, who died in 927.   But whatever our inscription means, it certainly does not say that Maelbrighde wrote this book.   The resemblance of the writing to that of the Book of Armagh (c. 807) has been thought to suggest a date not later than the middle of the ninth century.

Now Maelbrighde, son of Tornan, was a famous man.   As coarb (or heir) of St Patrick he ruled the abbey of Armagh for nearly forty years (888–927).[2]   He was also abbot of Hy (Iona) and of Raphoe.[3]   In 913, we are told, he went to Munster to release a pilgrim of the Britons.[4]   His death is thus recorded by the Four Masters (925 for 927) :

St Maelbrighde, son of Tornan, successor of Patrick, Colum Cille and Adamnan, head of the piety of all Ireland and of the greater part of Europe, died at a good old age, on the 22nd of February; in commemoration of whose death it was said:

On the eighth of the Calends of noble March
Maelbrighde, most gifted of the brave Gaedhil (died).
Premature the death of the abbot of Ard-Macha,
Maelbrighde, head of Europe.

[1] See *The Story of St Chad's Gospels*, by H. E. Savage, Dean of Lichfield, p. 3 (reprinted from *Trans. of Birmingham Archaeol. Soc.* xli (1915)), where illustrations are given of these pages in the Book of Kells and St Chad's Gospels.

[2] Lawlor and Best, *Coarbs of Patrick* (Proc. of Royal Irish Acad. xxxv, c, 9, p. 327).

[3] Reeves, *Adamn. Vita Columb.*, p. 392.

[4] *Ann. Ulst.* 912 (for 913), *Four Masters*, 908.

The name Maelbrighde was not uncommon.[1] It means the tonsured or devotee of Brigit, and is sometimes Latinized as *Calvus Brigidae*.[2]

Thus much for the famous man, 'head of the piety of all Ireland and of the greater part of Europe,' whose Gospel Book came into the hands of our K. Athelstan, whom the Ulster Annalist describes as 'the pillar of dignity of the Western world'.[3] Let us now look at the dedicatory inscription. It is all written in one hand, by an English scribe, and doubtless in Athelstan's lifetime. It falls into two parts, each preceded by a cross: it is alliterative and rhythmical,[4] after the fashion of some Anglo-Saxon charters.

✠ Mæielbrithus Mac Durnani
  istum textum per triquadrum
  deo digne dogmatizat.
✠ Ast Aethelstanus Anglosæxana
  rex et rector Doruuernensi
  metropoli dat per ævum.

No one seems to have found the explanation of the first triplet, though, as we have said, it has

[1] This was the name of Marianus Scotus, who left Ireland and became a recluse at Fulda and then at Maintz, and who wrote the Universal Chronicle which Florence of Worcester made the basis of his work; he died in 1082.

[2] Gilbert, *Facs. of Irish MSS*. I. xviii.

[3] *Ann. Ulst.* 938 (for 939).

[4] This was pointed out to me by Dr Savage, Dean of Lichfield, who suggests that the unusual word 'Ast' stands outside the rhythm, linking or contrasting the two parts. The scribe who was given this to copy has neglected to indicate the rhythmical structure.

been taken to indicate that Maelbrighde was the writer of the book. The puzzle of the piece is 'per triquadrum'. The solution is offered by two sentences from K. Athelstan's charters (B. C. S. 663, 667). The former was granted at Exeter in 928, and begins 'Afflante per cunctam triquadri orbis latitudinem'. The latter is dated 930, and its proëm says that the bounty of Providence has honoured Athelstan king of Albion with his father's throne and with surpassing fame throughout the wide world ('ac triquadri orbis rumigerula prae ceteris ampliavit praerogativa'). The 'tripartite world' is a rhetorical phrase: as we might speak of 'the two hemispheres'. Ducange throws no light on *triquadrus*: but in the Supplement two late and obscure references are given for 'triquadrus orbis'. More interesting is the fact, observed by Dr Savage (who arrived independently at the same solution), that Aldhelm is the source of this, as no doubt of other strange phrases of the charters. Thus we read in *De laudibus virginitatis* xviii 'triquadra mundi latitudo'; and in *De aris* xi 'Quae modo per mundum divulgant scripta triquadrum.' [1]

The next phrase, *deo digne*, is simply taken from the Vulgate, where it comes three times in the Epistles.[2] Lastly, *dogmatizat* means no more

---

[1] As Aldhelm more than once cites Orosius, we can trace his use of the phrase back to the *Historiae adversum paganos*, i. 2, where we read 'Majores nostri orbem totius terrae, oceani limbo circumsaeptum, triquadrum statuere, ejusque tres partes Asiam, Europam et Africam vocaverunt.'

[2] Col. i. 10, 1 Thes. ii. 12, 3 John 6.

than 'teaches' or 'proclaims'.[1] *Dogmatista* occurs not infrequently for a teacher.[2]

We see that we are dealing with one of Athelstan's scribes or literary men, and that this curious jumble of words means that Maelbrighde Mac Durnan 'right worthily proclaims this Gospel through the wide world', but K. Athelstan gives it to Christ Church, Canterbury, for ever. How did Athelstan come by the book of the abbot of Armagh? Did 'the head of the piety of all Ireland and of the greater part of Europe' come to the court of 'the pillar of dignity of the Western world', on his way perhaps to visit his Irish brethren in their continental monasteries, and leave his precious codex behind him in return for some right royal gift? We cannot tell: we must be satisfied with this fresh glimpse of our princely collector of sacred treasures.

Another gift of K. Athelstan to Christ Church, Canterbury, has a historical interest of a very different kind. Otto, son of Henry the king of the Saxons—one day to be famous as Otto the Great, the restorer of the Frankish Empire—had married one of Athelstan's sisters in the year 929. He came to the throne in 936, some three years before Athelstan's death. The English king may have sent him a congratulatory gift, and have received in return a copy of the Gospels which has on its twenty-third leaf the inscriptions ✠ ODDA REX

[1] Cf. B. C. S. 883 'Æþelpald (*for* Ælfpald) praesul pontificale cum augusto eulogium jubilando dogmatizavi.'

[2] Cf. B. C. S. 937, in the attestation, 'Dunstan dogmatista.'

and ✠ MIHTHILD MATER REGIS. The book is now in the British Museum as *Tiberius* A 2. Mr Edmund Bishop concluded from its *capitulare evangeliorum* that it was a product of the school of Lobbes, an abbey in the diocese of Liège. Lobbes was the home from time to time of the restless and vehement scholar-bishop, Ratherius of Verona, who became the tutor of Otto's brother Bruno, the learned and saintly archbishop of Cologne. K. Athelstan presented the book to Christ Church; and on f. 14 there are twenty lines of Latin verse commemorating the gift. More interesting is the dedication, of which we must note the opening and closing sentences: [1]

> Volumen hoc euuangelii ÆÐELSTAN Anglorum basyleos et curagulus totius Bryttannie devota mente Dorobernensis cathedre primatui tribuit ecclesiae Christo dicatae . . . Vos etenim obsecrando postulo memores ut vestris mei mellifluis oraminibus consonaque voce fieri, prout confido, non desistatis.

This lofty and quasi-imperial style ('basileos et curagulus') is peculiar to Athelstan.[2] In a contemporary charter of 939 (B. C. S. 734) he is called 'rex Anglorum et aeque totius Bryttanniae curagulus'; and a like description, generally with 'basileos' for 'rex', occurs in six other charters of less certain authenticity between 935 and 939. It would seem to have been assumed after his Northern expedition of 934.

[1] B. C. S. 710, 711.
[2] B. C. S. 952 in which Edmund is styled 'curagulus multarum gencium' is a forgery.

To St Augustine's abbey in Canterbury K. Athelstan presented a Gospel Book (Reg. I A xviii), which is said by the authorities at the British Museum to have been written probably in France early in the tenth century. Its dedication runs thus:

Hunc codicem ÆÐELSTAN rex devota mente Dorobernensi tribuit ecclesie beato Augustino dicate; et quisquis hoc legerit omnipotenti pro eo proque suis fundat preces

When we compare this with the dedication of the Christ Church book (*Tib.* A 2), we are struck by the recurrence of the phrases 'devota mente' and 'tribuit ecclesiae . . . dicatae'. There does not seem reason to suppose that this is due simply to the employment of a common form.

A more striking parallel to this dedication, though not to the same portions of it, is found in a book which Athelstan presented to the monastery of Bath. This is a ninth-century manuscript (*Claud.* B 5), containing the Acts of the Sixth General Council, held in 680. Here we read:

Hunc codicem Ætheltsanus (*sic*) rex tradidit deo et alme Christi genetrici sanctisque Petro et Benedicto in Bathonie civitatis coenobio, ob remunerationem suae animae; et quisquis hos legerit caracteres omnipotenti pro eo proque suis amicis fundat preces.

Not only do the two dedications begin in the same way, but the final clause in each is almost identically the same. Can this possibly be accounted for as 'common form'? Or must we not suppose that the same mind has dictated both?

In connexion with the Bath dedication a his-

torical point of no small importance must be noted.
The gift is made to God and Our Lady and the
saints Peter and Benedict.   The patron saints of
the church of Bath are St Peter and St Paul.   Can
we suppose that in K. Athelstan's time so prominent a place would have been assigned to St Benedict ?   The history of the monastery at that period
is very dim.   We have a charter of K. Athelstan
to the *familia* at Bath, but it is an obvious
forgery.[1]   From a foreign annalist we learn that,
when some of the monks at St Bertin retired from
their monastery rather than submit to the reforms
introduced by Gerard of Brogne, K. Athelstan
received them hospitably and gave them the
monastery of Bath.[2]   But the event is assigned to
the year 944, when Athelstan was dead and had
been succeeded by his brother Edmund.   Our
English sources tell us nothing of these refugees:
but the story suggests that this monastery like
many others was in the king's hand with but
a few clerks to serve the church.   And this is borne
out by the fact that in K. Edwy's time it was ruled,
not by an abbot, but by Wulfgar the king's mass-
priest.[3]   The reform reached it soon after, and no
doubt through Archbishop Dunstan, whose care
for the monks of Bath is attested by a story in
his Life.[4]

There is not the least reason to doubt that this

[1] B. C. S. 670.

[2] *Folcwini Gesta Abbatum S. Bertini*, Pertz. Mon. Germ.
xiii. 628.

[3] B. C. S. 927.

[4] *Memorials of St Dunstan* (R.S.), p. 46.

book was given to the church of Bath by K. Athelstan. The question before us is whether the dedication, which includes the name of St Benedict, can be supposed to be contemporary with the gift, or must not on historical grounds be referred to some writer of K. Edgar's day after the great reform. The problem is complicated by the remarkable parallels in phraseology between this dedication and those of the two Canterbury books just mentioned. These parallels suggest that a single mind has dictated them all. If we look to the time of K. Edgar as the earliest date of the Bath dedication, we should at once find the inspiring mind in Archbishop Dunstan, who had close relations with the three houses of Christ Church, St Augustine's, and Bath. We might think of him as desiring to make a permanent record of the gifts of his royal master, and to record the obligation of prayer on his behalf and on behalf of his friends who had been Dunstan's friends as well. Who, again, was more likely than Dunstan to recall Athelstan's title of 'Guardian of the whole of Britain'? The alternative explanation is that the three dedications were written about the same time at Athelstan's direction by scribes of his court: and this would be the obvious explanation but for the mention of St Benedict's name.

It will naturally be asked, what is the evidence of palaeography? Expert advice assures me that it is inconclusive. Nor is this surprising, when our question is whether certain notes were written (say) in 939 or in 964—a difference of but 25 years. To take the details: (1) The Bath dedication might have been written at either date; (2) the St Augustine's dedication, which is so strikingly similar, has a later look and could even be attributed to the beginning of the eleventh century; (3) the Christ Church book has first a dedication in verse in a minuscule hand of the first part of the tenth century, and then the prose dedication, with which we are concerned, in a more distinctly insular script which may be of much the same date. Palaeography therefore will not enable us to decide whether the mention of St Benedict in connexion with Bath can be safely referred to the days of K. Athelstan.

From Bath we pass to Winchester. Here we have to do with the remarkable manuscript (*Galba* A 18) which is known as the Athelstan Psalter. This manuscript was at Winchester at the time of the suppression of the monasteries, and came into the possession of Thomas Dackombe a member of the new cathedral foundation. It was then known as 'Psalterium regis Athelstani', either as having been Athelstan's own book of devotions, or as having been given by him to the Old Minster with words of dedication now lost. The Psalter was written on the Continent in the ninth century; but the chief interest of the book consists in certain additional matter inserted after it came to England and written in the early part of the tenth century. Thus it contains the Apostles' Creed, the Lord's Prayer, the Trisagion, and a short Litany of the Saints—all in the Greek language, but in Latin letters. This Litany is of exceptional importance as the starting-point of a long development: it probably came into England from Rome at the end of the seventh century, when the pope was Sergius, a Greek, whose interest in liturgical matters is well attested. Moreover this manuscript contains the earliest of three known copies of a metrical calendar directly connected with the English royal house. This, no less than the Litany just referred to, has been carefully investigated by Mr Edmund Bishop.[1] It has a line for every day of the year. Some of these verses are plainly of Irish origin, but the basis of the calendar is not Irish. Mr Bishop sums up the matter thus:

It would appear then that we have in our metrical calendar the production of one of those nameless Scotti mentioned by Asser, who found their way to Alfred's court; and, though it cannot in our sense be considered an Irish document, but rather English, it is in the highest degree interesting as the only liturgical document that comes down to us from Alfred's times or the early days of Edward the Elder; and from the point of view both of liturgy and of Alfred it deserves much more attention than it has hitherto received.

It only remains to be said that the grandparents of K. Athelstan are thus recorded: on 26 October, the death of Alfred:

Aelfred rex obiit septenis et quoque Amandus;

and on 8 December, the death of his queen Ealhswith:

Quinta tenet veram dominam Anglorum Ealhswithe.

Besides the gift-books of which we have spoken

[1] *Liturgica Historica*, 140 ff., 254 ff.

there are several other manuscripts which for various reasons contain K. Athelstan's name.

(1) Reg. 1 B vii is an eighth-century book of the Gospels, closely akin to the Lindisfarne (or St Cuthbert's) Gospels. These two books are nearly contemporaneous with the famous Codex Amiatinus of Jarrow, and present the same valuable Northumbrian text of the Vulgate. Moreover they both give the Neapolitan lists of liturgical feasts, which have been so fully discussed of late in Dom Chapman's *Early History of the Vulgate Gospels*. Our immediate interest in the codex (Reg. 1 B vii) lies in an entry on f. 15b of a manumission granted by K. Athelstan 'immediately after he became king'. I have discussed this entry elsewhere,[1] and it will come before us again when we speak of K. Athelstan as a collector of relics.

Now Wanley in his Catalogue supposed this MS to have come into the British Museum from Christ Church, Canterbury, but gave no reason for his view. Dr M. R. James, on the other hand, prefers to think that it belonged to St Augustine's. If we adopt this latter view, we may allow ourselves to indulge in a conjecture which would lead to the answer to two puzzling questions. First, why does an entry of a manumission made 'immediately after' Athelstan became king come to be in this important codex of the Gospels? And, secondly, why did the abbey of St Augustine, as we learn from its great Register,[2] receive from K. Athelstan on the actual day of his coronation (4 September

[1] *The Saxon Bishops of Wells*, p. 32.
[2] *Ibid.*, p. 31.

925) a charter restoring to it certain lands in Thanet ? Both questions are answered if this was the very Gospel Book on which K. Athelstan took the solemn oath of his coronation, and if it had been borrowed for the purpose by Archbishop Athelm from the monks of St Augustine's abbey. Manumissions were frequently entered for greater security in the Gospel Books of important churches; and the monks of St Augustine's may well have received a boon in return, if they had lent their valuable book for use at the coronation.

This will be a convenient place to notice the poem on K. Athelstan, which is found in *Nero* A 2 in a very corrupt text. In 1909 Mr C. H. Turner found a fragment of the same poem in a yet more corrupt text at Durham;[1] and in July 1911 Mr W. H. Stevenson made the interesting discovery that the poem was based on a much older one addressed to Charles the Great, and he was thus able to restore it to a less unintelligible form.[2] 'It is', he says, 'a greeting from some over-sea poet, probably a resident in Frankland.' It refers to the events of 926 or 927, and may have been written when K. Athelstan's glories were spread abroad, together with his princely gifts, by the mission of Bishop Coenwald of Worcester to the monasteries of Germany in 929.

The MS (*Nero* A 2) is dated by Mr Stevenson

---

[1] *Journ. of Theol. Studies*, x. 537: from Durh. A ii. 17, f. 31 *b* (at foot), ending 'Constantine'. This is a Gospel Book of cent. viii.

[2] *Eng. Hist. Review*, xxvi. 482.

about the middle of the tenth century. But this poem is preceded on the same gathering by a calendar which contains St Dunstan's name and cannot well be earlier than the beginning of the eleventh century. This calendar is described by Mr Edmund Bishop (*Bosworth Psalter*, pp. 152, 165 ff.). 'It is full of archaisms,' he tells us: 'it comes not merely from the most remote but from the most Celtic, backward, part of the country— the furthermost Wessex; and gives probably the type of calendar existing in Devonshire before Leofric, with his foreign education, took the Church of these parts in hand.' The presence of the poem, therefore, in such a manuscript is another link between K. Athelstan and Devon.

The poem is immediately followed by what is called the Prayer of K. Athelstan. The only reason for this attribution would seem to be its position in the manuscript, taken in conjunction with the fact that the last line but one of the poem begins with 'Dixit rex Æthelstanus': but this Mr Stevenson has shown to be a corruption of 'Dic ut rex Æthelstanus'. The Prayer is found again, and is followed by an English version, in *Galba* A 14, a book of prayers written in the tenth and eleventh centuries, which has been described by Mr Edmund Bishop (*Liturgica Historica*, 384–95) and assigned to the Nunnaminster at Winchester. It is a prayer for victory, and the passage referring to David and Goliath forms part of a litany in another Winchester book of prayers of the eighth or ninth century.[1]

[1] Harl. 7653: Birch, 'An Ancient Manuscript,' Hants Rec. Soc., app., p. 116.

It must suffice here to make a passing reference to the entry of K. Athelstan's name in the three Swiss Confraternity Books of St Gall, Reichenau, and Pfäfers. I have discussed these entries at some length elsewhere.[1]

I have left to the last two MSS which have found a home in Oxford.

1. Bodl. *Rawl.* C 697: a tenth-century codex containing works of Aldhelm and Prudentius. It belonged at one time to St Edmund's monastery at Bury. At the end is a strange and untranslateable acrostic, the first letters of which make 'Adalstan' and the last letters 'Johannes'.[2]

2. C. C. C. Oxon. 122: a Gospel Book in an Irish hand, with a few notes in Irish, said to be of the end of the eleventh century. It has the Eusebian Canons (ff. 1*b*–5*a*), followed on f. 5*b* by a scheme

---

[1] *The Saxon Bishops of Wells*, pp. 60 ff.

[2]
  A rchalis clamare triumvir nomine sax i
  D ive tuo fors prognossim feliciter aev o
  A ugustae.Samu.cernentis rupis eris.el. h
  L arvales forti beliales robure contr a
  S aepe seges messem fęcunda praenotat altam i n
  T utis solandum petrinum solibus agme n
  A mplius amplificare sacra sophismatis arc e
  N omina orto petas donet precor inclita doxu s

To any one whose curiosity is aroused by this poem I can offer no more than the following: *Archalis saxi* and *Augustae rupis* represent the name 'Æthelstan'; *clamare* and *amplificare* seem to be 2nd pers. sing. pres. passive; the *h* of *Samuhel* is transposed for an obvious reason: *cernentis* may be for *videntis* which is used in the Vulgate for 'Samuel the Seer'; the last line seems intended for *Petas, precor, donet orthodoxus inclita nomina.*

summarizing the Canons, and also by a Table ruled like a chess-board with 324 squares, 18 on a side: the squares, however, are not alternately black and white, but all alike plain. Square black pieces—'men' (*viri*) as they are called—are set, not in the middle of the squares, but at points where four squares meet. The pieces are scattered thinly at the corners of the board, but there is a circle of them towards the middle, and within this a smaller group close round the centre. Above this Table is the following title:

Alea Evangelii [the Game, or Playing-board, of the Gospel], which Dubinsi bishop of Bangor brought away from the king of the English, that is, from the house of Adelstan king of the English; depicted by a certain Frank and a Roman sage, that is, Israel.

If any one would know this game (*aleam*) fully, before all the lessons of this teaching (*hujus disciplinae documenta*) he must thoroughly know (*scire animo*) these seven: to wit, dukes and counts, defenders and attackers, city and citadel, and nine steps (*gradus*) twice over.

The Table is followed by an explanation which occupies the next two pages, and begins: 'A Roman Jew and a Frank, men most skilled in the Four Gospels'; and goes on to explain in elaborate detail the meaning of the pieces and their positions on the board. Now the Four Masters tell us under the year 951 (for 953) that 'Duibhinnsi, a sage and bishop of the family of Beannchair' died: and the Annals of Ulster have a similar entry.[1] Dubinsi, then, was a monastic bishop under the abbot of

---

[1] *Four Masters*, ed. O'Donovan (1856), ii. 669: the *Ann. Ulst.* are there quoted in a note.

Bangor in Ireland. What brought him to K. Athelstan's court we cannot tell: perhaps he was travelling with Maelbrighde the great abbot of Armagh.

I have to thank Mr Plummer and the librarian of Corpus Christi College for arranging that the MS should be sent to the Bodleian, where I have transcribed the whole passage with the skilled assistance of Mr Gambier Parry.[1] Both the Table and its explanation have suffered somewhat from the inaccuracy of the eleventh-century copyist; but the meaning can be made out, and it is somewhat disappointing. For all that we get is the reason why there should be 72 pieces or 'men', and why these 'men' are placed at particular points of the board. The pieces are set: but the players are gone, and how the game was played must remain a mystery to those who do not know all about the 'dukes and counts, defenders and attackers, city and citadel, and nine steps twice over.' Some ancient form of chess or draughts may one day give the key to the problem. What is of interest to us is that somebody knew about it in K. Athelstan's marvellous court, whence Dubinsi 'the sage and bishop' fetched it away to Ireland in those far-off spacious days.

A Collector of Relics

The subject of Relics may seem unprofitable to the student of history. Yet the places they came from, and the people who gave or stored them, the various uses to which they were put, and the

---

[1] See below, Additional Note D.

strange tricks that were played with them—all these have something to tell us of the life and habits of mind of a generation which did great things for the making of England. Of the healing powers of certain relics modern thought is less incredulous than it was. The solemnity of an oath depended greatly on the relics upon which it was sworn, and in Frankland at any rate it was well to assure yourself beforehand that the relics were in the chests which were supposed to contain them, or your enemy's oath 'super vacuas capsas' might cost you your life.[1] The relic-hunter seemed to enjoy a peculiar exemption from the common code of honesty: the saint who allowed himself to be surreptitiously removed was held to be dissatisfied with his former custodians; and the Abingdon monks unblushingly put on record that a certain batch of holy bones had been stolen from Glastonbury.[2]

K. Athelstan has a unique record among monarchs as a collector of relics. One of the two earliest documents of his reign is a manumission 'immediately after he became king', written into a Gospel Book to which we have already referred.[3] At the end the king says: 'May he who alters this incur the wrath of God and of all the *haligdom* that I have gotten me into England by God's mercy.' It is just possible, as we have suggested, that this Gospel Book may have been used at his

[1] Cf. Fredegarius, *Continuatio*, c. xcvii; *Gesta Regum Francorum*, c. 46 (apud Bouquet, ii. 451, 570).

[2] *Hist. Abingd.* R. S. App. II, p. 280.

[3] Reg. I B. vii: see above, p. 66.

coronation, and that the *haligdom*, or collection of sacred relics, may also have been brought for the king to swear his oath upon. When we pass from his coronation to his funeral the same thing meets us: 'There were borne before his corpse', says William of Malmesbury in whose abbey it lay, 'the relics of saints which he had purchased from Britain beyond the sea.'[1]

The mention of Brittany recalls the letter of Radbod, the prior of St Samson's at Dol, written to the king some time before 927:

Your father Edward, while our land was still at peace, entered into confraternity with our house. We still pray for his soul, and also for your welfare. Grateful for your kindness I and my twelve canons promise to pray day and night. I send you relics, which we know you value more than earthly treasure—bones of St Senator, and of St Paternus and his master St Scabillion, who died on the same day as he. These two lay right and left of St Paternus: their solemnities like his are on the ninth of the Kalends of October. We who are exiles in France beg you to remember us.

So, in brief, the letter runs. These poor canons had fled before the Northmen who had devastated Brittany in the reign of K. Athelstan's father. They had carried off their saints with them and had found refuge in France. K. Athelstan had been kind to them, and they wished to show their gratitude by sending him a few of their most precious bones. William of Malmesbury tells us that the bones of St Paternus (St Pair, bishop of Avranches) were given to Malmesbury. Probably

[1] *Gesta Regum*, R. S., i. 157.

the others went to Middleton (Milton Abbas) in Dorset, which K. Athelstan had founded, and where this letter was discovered in a shrine.[1] The Middleton register informs us that K. Athelstan gave to that abbey part of the true Cross, an arm and bones of St Samson, as well as his crozier; an arm of St Branwalador; and many other relics in five shrines still firmly closed: all which relics he bought from the holy Roman Church and from Britain beyond the sea.[2]

When we glance at the history of Brittany, we learn from the Chronicle of Nantes that Alan the Great, who had kept the Northmen out of his country, died in 907. When they over-ran it in 919, a vast multitude of refugees crossed the Channel. Among them was Alan, afterwards known as Twisted Beard, the grandson of Alan the Great. He was godson to Athelstan and was brought up from childhood at his court. It would seem that after various efforts to save his country he came again to England in 931. Then in 936 by Athelstan's aid he made a successful expedition and became duke of Brittany in the following year.[3]

Tokens of this immigration have been found by the late Dr McLure in the inscribed stones in the church at Wareham.[4] And Mr Edmund Bishop has said that Winchester documents of the tenth and eleventh centuries 'witness to a veritable

---

[1] *Gesta Pontif.* (R. S.), 399 f.
[2] *Monasticon*, ii. 349 f.
[3] *Chron. Namnet* ed. Merlet, pp. 80 ff., 88.
[4] *British Place Names*, p. 161.

devotional *furore* in Bretonism'. After referring to some litanies, he adds that the evidence goes to show 'that the presence of the distinctly Breton element in the Winchester calendar of the eleventh century is probably due to Athelstan, and that the Breton cults at Winchester date from his reign'.[1]

Nothing could seem a less promising field for research than the Lists of Relics preserved in some of our greatest churches. Nevertheless we will make trial of one or two, beginning with Westminster. John Flete, who was prior of Westminster Abbey about 1460, has given us such a list.[2] Our interest is not in the relics themselves so much as in their donors, amongst whom we find K. Sebert, the somewhat mythical founder of the abbey, and the great kings Offa, Athelstan, Edgar, and the rest. We will not stop to ask whether the relics were what they professed to be, or even whether it is certain that these kings actually gave them. What matters is that as we turn the pages of list after list of our English monasteries we find Athelstan among the greatest of the donors. Here at Westminster we read that 'K. Athelstan gave part of the Cross and of the Sepulchre of the Lord, and portions of the Mount of Olives and of Mount Sinai': 'K. Athelstan gave a certain veil of the Holy Virgin Mary': 'K. Athelstan gave relics of the apostles Peter, Bartholomew, Andrew and Barnabas': 'K. Athelstan

---

[1] *Bosworth Psalter*, p. 56.

[2] Westminster Notes and Documents: no. 2, *Flete's History of Westminster*, pp. 68–73.

granted relics of the holy martyrs Laurence, Hippolytus, Tiburtius, Valerian, Quintin, with others': 'K. Athelstan gave relics of Batildis, Martina and other holy virgins'.

Now it was not till Athelstan had been in his grave for twenty years that St Dunstan took Westminster in hand, and brought monks, probably from Glastonbury, to dwell there. Till then there was but a small church there of no significance. Dunstan himself is not among the donors of relics—indeed his recorded gifts to churches usually take the form of books or bells or organs: but it is possible that he had part of K. Athelstan's treasury of relics at his disposal, and may have given some of the items mentioned in his old master's name. But Flete has more to tell us. He gives what he calls the First Charter of K. Edward the Confessor, the next great founder of the abbey. This bears the date 28 December 1065. It is most certainly not genuine, but it preserves an interesting tradition. St Edward is made to say that, when he built the new church at Westminster and caused it to be consecrated, he made the following gift:[1] 'I placed there on that day relics which Pope Marinus and Leo the pope who consecrated K. Alfred gave to that king, and relics which he himself had desired Carloman king of the Franks to give him, when his father K. Ethelwulf after his first wife's decease married Carloman's daughter: which relics came from Alfred to his successor Athelstan, and then to

[1] Westminster Notes and Documents: no. 2, *Flete's History of Westminster*, p. 52.

Edgar, and last of all to me: namely, two parts of the Lord's Cross and part of one nail, and part 'of His garment that was all of one piece throughout; and portions of the garment of St Mary, and relics of the apostles Peter and Paul, Andrew, Bartholomew, Barnabas, and many other saints; and five cases filled with other relics of saints'.

Here is a list of some of the Westminster relics, which comes probably from the days of K. Stephen. It corresponds in part with the later list of Flete's own time. We note that Athelstan's name gets a passing notice in what we may call the genealogy of the relics—perhaps because some of the relics had labels which connected them with him. Two points attract our attention. 'Five cases filled with other relics of saints' have come down among the royal donations. We are reminded of the 'five cases firmly closed' that were kept at Middleton Abbey. Then we have Pope Marinus. No doubt his name comes directly or indirectly from the Anglo-Saxon Chronicle which tells us (in all copies except A, strangely enough) under the year 883 that Pope Marinus sent K. Alfred a piece of the wood of the Cross. What Alfred did with it is another question. When William of Malmesbury was writing his book on the Antiquity of the Church of Glastonbury about 1135, the only gift that he could discover to have been made to that abbey by K. Alfred was a piece of the wood of the Cross.[1] We must however remember that a very little of that sacred relic was made to go a great way,

[1] Hearne's *Adam of Domerham*, i. 70.

and it is not at all unlikely that Glastonbury only got a fragment of what the pope sent to the king.

As our story has brought us to Glastonbury, let us take a glance at the relic list of that great house. 'Innumerable relics', says William of Malmesbury, 'and of high excellence' were given by K. Athelstan, 'as is noted in the Textus of St Dunstan.'[1] The book thus referred to would be a Gospel Book, said to have been given by St Dunstan, with a splendid binding made by that skilled artificer. Two lists have come down to us, one arranged by chests, the other classified according to subjects.[2] Thirty items of relics connected with Our Lord are attributed to K. Athelstan, whereas only three or four are noted as given at a later time. This is probably the result of some confusion: but it shows at any rate that Athelstan was thought of as a great collector of such things.

I shall not trouble you with the Exeter relics: the list comes from the Leofric Missal, and claims rather too boldly a third of all the relics that K. Athelstan brought from abroad.[3]

To the Old Church at Winchester K. Athelstan gave the head of St Justus the martyr, as is noted under the year 924 in the Winchester Annals.[4] As to the New Minster the matter is not very clear. In the *Liber Vitae*, edited by Dr Birch,[5] we find

[1] Hearne's *Adam of Domerham,* i. 71.

[2] Hearne's *John of Glaston.* ii. 445–54, i. 22 ff.

[3] The English Text is in B. C. S. 693: the same with a translation into Latin may be read in the *Monasticon,* ii. 528 ff.

[4] *Ann. Winton.* (R. S.), p. 24: cf. Edm. Bishop, *Lit. Hist.,* p. 399.   [5] pp. lxv, 162 f.

a heading: 'This is the *halidom* that is in the shrine that Alwold the church-ward wrought.' It begins thus: 'This is all the *halidom* that was with King Athelstan's gems.' So Dr Birch explains the words *on Æþelstanes kyningces gimma*. I do not feel certain about this rendering, as the passage continues: 'and bones of St Sebastian', and so on. At any rate we have here also evidence of K. Athelstan's zeal in this kind.

Lastly we come to Abingdon. We have already said that in Athelstan's time this was a derelict monastery, whose possessions had for the most part been taken over by K. Alfred, a small estate being left to a few clerks who served the church. Now the poem from which William of Malmesbury drew most of his account of the glories of K. Athelstan told in picturesque style of an embassy which came to Abingdon, where a court was being held, to ask the hand of one of the king's sisters for Hugh the Great, duke of France.[1] It was led by Adulf (Adalolf), the brother of Count Arnulf of Flanders and lay-abbot of St Bertin's abbey at St Omer. This was the more appropriate, since his mother Ealswith had been K. Alfred's daughter. As the marriage of Ethilda to Duke Hugh took place in 926, it is possible that the embassy arrived early in that year. K. Athelstan's proclivities were doubtless already well known on the Continent; for, besides a multitude of costly presents, an astonishing treasure of relics was offered to the king:

---

[1] *Gesta Regum*, i. p. 150: he says in error 'Hugo rex'.

1. The sword of Constantine the Great, with one
   of the nails of the Cross set in gold in the
   hilt;
2. The lance of Charlemagne, which was that
   wherewith the Centurion had pierced the
   Lord's side;
3. The standard of St Maurice, the captain of
   the Theban legion;
4. A portion of the Cross set in crystal;
5. A portion of the Crown of Thorns, similarly
   enclosed.

Part of the Cross and of the Crown of Thorns
went to Malmesbury, as William tells us: the
other relics were preserved to enrich the king's
successors.

The mention of Abingdon in this connexion did
not escape the notice of its monks of a later time.[1]
They give their own account of the occasion,
which they naturally enough describe as the king's
Easter court; and they add that the abbot at the
time was Godescale, the successor of Abbot
Cynath.   We have dealt with these imagined
abbots already.[2]   What remains to be said is that
the Abingdon treasury claimed to possess part of
the Crown of Thorns, part of a nail of the Cross,
the standard of St Maurice, and a finger of St
Denys: all these were given by K. Athelstan in
a silver chest.   Of this we need only remark that
it was a bold claim.

[1] *Hist. Abingd.* i. 88; cf. ii. 276 and note.
[2] See above, p. 36.

IV

ST DUNSTAN

In one of the south windows of the south transept at Wells there still remains a small piece of ancient glass on which is figured a mitred saint, holding an archiepiscopal cross in his left hand, while with the tongs in his right hand he takes the devil by the nose. This famous exploit, of which we first hear a hundred years after his death, has been the ruin of Dunstan's reputation. If we add to it the false tales of his cruelty, invented by spiteful controversialists in the sixteenth century, we have the whole of what the ordinary Englishman of education can tell you to-day of one of the greatest of his countrymen. He was, nevertheless, one of the makers of England. Alfred, Athelstan and Dunstan—'these three' were 'mighty men':[1] of all the rest that were before the Norman Conquest it must be written that 'they attained not unto the first three'. Alfred stood in the last ditch against the Danes at Athelney, reorganized the State, and brought back learning to the Church. Athelstan, after his victory at Brunanburh, could with justice style himself *basileus* of all Britain': foreign princes sought his alliance, and many links were formed between England and the wider civilization of Europe. Dunstan was the strong and prudent guide of three young

[1] 2 Sam. xxiii. 17 ff.

kings, Edmund, Edred, and Edgar the Peaceful, the last of whom owes his fame largely to this great archbishop, whom we may fairly call the first prime minister of England, great alike as statesman, reformer, and saint.

Dunstan was born at Baltonsborough (pronounced Balsbury), four miles out of Glastonbury, about ten years after K. Alfred's death, and just at the time that his uncle Athelm became the first bishop of Wells: let us say in the year 909. He was connected with the royal family, and the court was much in Somerset in those days. His education he got at Glastonbury, 'the royal island', as it was called. The abbey appears to have been for some time in the king's hands, ruled, it may be, by thanes who were abbots only in name. Religious observance was low, and not much learning was to be found there; but it was still a centre to which Irish pilgrims came, and Dunstan profited by their knowledge and their books. In 923 his uncle Athelm left Wells for Canterbury, and at the end of the next year K. Edward died and was succeeded by K. Athelstan. The boy Dunstan followed Athelm to Canterbury, and was commended by him to the care of the newly crowned king. Soon after this Archbishop Athelm died.

At K. Athelstan's court were two priests, serving as chaplains and writers of his charters, both of whom bore the same name. One was called Ælfheah the priest, the other, for the sake of distinction, Ælfheah the priest and monk: sometimes the latter had to be content with a less pleasing designation, and history knows him best

as Ælfheah the Bald.[1]   The first Ælfheah became
bishop of Wells, when Wulfhelm, who had succeeded Athelm there, passed on to succeed him
also at Canterbury.   The second Ælfheah was
a kinsman of Dunstan, and like him was connected
with the royal house: probably he was a Somerset
man and a monk of Glastonbury.   About 934 he
became bishop of Winchester.   Dunstan was then
some twenty-five years old, and was still undecided
as to his course of life.

Athelstan's court—who shall describe that for
us?   We must not think of it as fixed in one place,
such as Winchester.   It was constantly on the
move, and often, as we have said, in Somerset.
It was the refuge of youthful princes from abroad.
One of them was to wear the crown of France, and
to be called Louis d'Outremer in memory of his
exile across the sea; another was Alan, K. Athelstan's god-son, waiting to be old enough to fight
his way back to his lost inheritance of Brittany;
and a third was young Haakon, of Norway, also
training for a throne.   When we recall, besides,
the foreign embassies which brought magnificent
presents to a king famed for his splendour and
bounty, we may conjecture what intercourse
England then had with the Continent, and what
treasures of art and literature arrived to stimulate
the energies of such a youth as Dunstan, clever at
writing and illuminating manuscripts, at music and
song, and at every kind of work in metals.   Hither
also came Howell the Good, wisest of Welsh kings;

[1] Is it possible that 'Calvus' was regarded as specially
appropriate to a monk?   Cf. above, p. 57.

and sometimes the treacherous Constantine, king of the restless Scotland. What a school of states- manship was here: what knowledge of the wider world was opened up to an inquiring mind!

Presently we find Dunstan back at Glastonbury, and the court somewhere in the neighbourhood. His book-learning made this dreamy youth un- popular with his companions and younger kinsmen. His fondness for the old Saxon songs and his mechanical skill were twisted into a charge of black arts. Slander prevailed and he was dis- missed from the court. Then he was attacked on the road by his young persecutors, who tied him up and flung him into the watery moor and trampled him in the mud. Barely escaping with his life, he reached a friend's house a mile away: the dogs flew at him in his muddy disguise, but quickly recognized him by his voice. There is a vivid touch of ancient Somerset in this, though we cannot fix the spot.

Next comes the crisis of his career. Bishop Ælfheah was urging him to become a monk, and he was not ready for the sacrifice, contrasting, we are told, the attractions of a married life with the austere garb of the cloister. A sharp illness brought him to a decision: the bishop came at his urgent entreaty, and on his recovery clothed him with the monastic habit. This may have been about the year 936; and not long afterwards Ælfheah ordained to the priesthood on the same day Dunstan the monk and his brilliant young friend Ethelwold, who like himself had been trained at K. Athelstan's court.

Athelstan's death in 939 brought Dunstan to the side of the young king Edmund as his chief counsellor. But once more envy poisoned the royal mind against him and secured his disgrace. He was arranging to leave the country with the ambassadors of a foreign prince whom the king chanced to be entertaining at Cheddar, when a strange incident occurred. K. Edmund was hunting a stag, which darted up through the woods to the top of Cheddar gorge. Seeing no way of escape it leapt over the cliff, followed by the baying hounds. The king saw his danger, but his horse was beyond his utmost power of control. The wrong done to Dunstan flashed through his mind, and he vowed to make him amends if his life were spared. On the very edge the horse stopped short and turned aside. When the king got home he sent for Dunstan, and made him ride with him to Glastonbury. There he set him in the abbot's seat and bade him rule the house he loved. It was a turning point in the history of religion in England, the beginning of the fulfilment of Dunstan's early dreams and Bishop Ælfheah's prayers.

Dunstan started to rebuild the monastery and make it a safe enclosure wherein he could train a body of monks in the strict observance of St Benedict's Rule. To free both himself and them from external distractions he made his brother Wulfric provost of the abbey estates, which began to be substantially increased by the generous gifts of the king and other benefactors. His friend Ethelwold joined him, first as a pupil, then as a monk; and soon he became his right hand in the government of the monastery. Then came those ten or, it may be, fifteen years of steady, quiet labour, which built up the fame of Glastonbury as the one school of true monastic life in England. Men of high birth and eager spirit were once more attracted to the cloister, and from Glastonbury in the following years came a continual stream of abbots and bishops, leaders of the great revival in the Church.

Meanwhile Edmund's assassination (946) called his brother Edred to the throne, and Abbot Dunstan was more than ever the steersman of the state. The king, who bravely fought against painful bodily infirmity, even as Alfred his grandfather had done before him, ruled well and would have rewarded Dunstan's services with a bishopric. But the abbot refused to leave his side so long as he lived. A large part of the royal treasure was in his keeping at Glastonbury, his counsel was needed at every turn, and a strong personal affection bound him to his 'most beloved' king. The end came soon afterwards, and in 955 the boy Edwy, Edmund's elder son, was chosen by both peoples—that is, to the joint rule of Wessex and Mercia. At once a reaction set in against the powerful minister, who with the good queen-mother had dominated the last two reigns. We need not repeat the wretched story of female intrigue: the property of the old queen was seized, and Dunstan was driven beyond the sea. He took refuge with Arnulf, count of Flanders— probably a kinsman, for Arnulf's mother was

K. Alfred's daughter. He found a welcome in the reformed monastery of Blandinium at Ghent.

It was time that the monastic reform in England should come into direct contact with the somewhat earlier movements of the like kind on the Continent. Cluny had been founded about the time of Dunstan's birth: Fleury had been reformed by an abbot of Cluny in 930. To Fleury, indeed, Oswald, a nephew of Oda the Good, who though a Dane had risen to be archbishop of Canterbury, was attracted by the fame of its religious observance: but Oswald did not return to England till his uncle's death in 958. To Fleury or some other foreign house Ethelwold had wished to go, but the queen-mother had warned Edred of the danger of losing him, and so he had been sent off with companions from Glastonbury to restore the ancient monastery of Abingdon. Thus it came about that Dunstan himself was the first effectual link between the revived English monasticism and the great continental reforms; and it was to a Lotharingian house, reformed not from Cluny but by the famous Gerard of Brogne, that the providence of his exile had brought him.

In 957 Mercia revolted against Edwy's misrule, and Edgar his younger brother was chosen as king of the country north of the Thames. He at once recalled Dunstan, who was made a bishop and ruled for a while the vacant sees of Worcester and London. Then, after Edwy's death in 959, the kingdoms were reunited under Edgar, and Dunstan became archbishop of Canterbury. The monastic movement now went forward rapidly. Oswald had returned from Fleury and was made bishop of Worcester. He started a small monastery at Westbury-on-Trym as a new centre of reform: presently Duke Ethelwin gave him Ramsey, where an important abbey was founded; and monks were then gradually settled in the cathedral church of Worcester. Ethelwold, who had made Abingdon a model house, became bishop of Winchester in 963. With K. Edgar's aid he expelled the clerks from the Old and the New Minsters, putting Abingdon monks in their place. This was a violent procedure, though we can hardly say it was unjustified, if what we are told of the clergy whom he found there is not a gross exaggeration. More praiseworthy is his work as the restorer of Ely, Peterborough, Thorney, and other ruined abbeys.

Archbishop Dunstan does **not** appear as taking an active part in these restorations, though Bath and Malmesbury and probably Westminster were reformed by him: but his was the controlling spirit, and to him was due the persistent activity of the king in forwarding the work. Above all, his influence is to be traced in the great code of Customs, called the *Regularis Concordia*, which prescribed those details of the monastic life by which the observance of St Benedict's Rule was carried out in practice. It was drawn up by Bishop Ethelwold, with the aid of monks brought over both from Fleury and from Ghent. It was the outcome of a synod held at Winchester, and was put forth in the king's name for all the English houses. Though full advantage was taken of the

wisdom and experience of foreigners, the document bears a national impress; the king and
queen appear as protectors and supervisors of
houses for men and women respectively; and the
repetition of prayers for king, queen, and royal
family, which is so marked a feature of our
services to-day, is as nothing when compared with
the number of prayers which were daily offered
on their behalf by the monks of the tenth century.
The effect of this code in the great process of the
unification of England under Edgar and Dunstan
is deserving of the historian's consideration. That
unification was the glory of Edgar's reign: it was
the issue of complete co-operation between the
Church and the State, and to Dunstan more than
to any other the credit of it must be given.[1]

After K. Edgar's death in 975 Dunstan, who
was now an old man, took a less prominent part
in affairs of state, and devoted himself more
exclusively to the spiritual work of his own diocese.
He had shown himself strong to rebuke kings,
and on one occasion he is recorded to have set
aside a letter from the pope, licensing a certain
action which he held to be wrong. 'Not a hair's
breadth', he declared, 'would he move from the
law of his Lord.' He was stern, but he was gentle
too, and full of kindness to the poor; and he
loved to gather the boys of the cloister about him
and tell them stories of the olden days. He passed
away on 19 May 988, with the Psalmist's words

[1] In illustration of this I would refer to my article on
'The Coronation Order in the Tenth Century' (*Journ. of
Theol. Studies*, October 1917, vol. xix, pp. 71 f.).

on his lips: 'The merciful and gracious Lord hath so done His marvellous works, that they ought to be had in remembrance.' For his greatness and his holiness the instinct of the English people at once acclaimed him as a saint.[1]

This outline of St Dunstan's career differs in some important points from the commonly accepted account, which has prevailed for the last half century owing to the great authority of the late Bishop Stubbs. He was one of the first writers to vindicate the character of the saint from the gross misrepresentations which had rendered him odious as a type of monkish fanaticism and cruelty. Already in 1862 John Richard Green had begun to do him justice, and spoke of him as 'the first of that great line of ecclesiastical statesmen who counted among them Lanfranc and Wolsey and Laud'.[2] In 1872 E. W. Robertson in his *Historical Essays* had gone farther in the same direction, using such materials as were then accessible. But to Stubbs's *Memorials of St Dunstan*, published for the Master of the Rolls in 1874, we owe not only a full collection of the documents which tell the story of his life, but also the fascinating introduction which has finally established his reputation as a statesman. But, while Bishop Stubbs is without rival as an exponent

[1] For this summary account it will suffice to make a general reference to the two pre-Conquest Lives of St Dunstan, edited by Bishop Stubbs in his *Memorials of St Dunstan* in the Rolls Series; and for some points of detail to my *Saxon Bishops of Wells*.

[2] In a paper on 'St Dunstan at Glastonbury' in the *Proceedings of the Somerset Archaeological Society*, XI, ii, 123.

of ecclesiastical policy, he was not an historian of religion and he had no sympathy with monks. There is something more to be said about Dunstan even after the fine historical portrait which that master hand has drawn. I can best express my meaning by a quotation from an article in the Dublin Review on *English Hagiology*, written as long ago as January 1885 by the late Mr Edmund Bishop.

The greatness of Dunstan's character, his political insight, his pre-eminently statesmanlike capacities, even his moderation, are allowed and insisted on. But it may be questioned whether the views now in vogue do not leave out of sight the most marked features of his character and habits of life. The institution of his religious cult immediately after his death, its almost universal diffusion throughout the country among his contemporaries, is a fact of the highest significance. It was neither the statesman, the prelate, the monk, nor the patriot—though he was all these—who was thus honoured and venerated, but the man in whom those who had conversed and acted with him, seen and known him, had recognized the features of unworldiness, humbleness of heart, and love of God, which in their minds were associated with the idea of a saint. This note is distinctly perceptible in the account given by his anonymous biographer—the more so when we compare it with the busy benevolence and the exterior religious pre-occupations set forth in the life of St Ethelwold. Thrown more than any other in the midst of the world and its cares, Dunstan walked in a sense alone, he felt the responsibilities imposed on him both by his position and his commanding character which necessarily made him a leader: others might rely upon him, he could lean on God alone. Recollection in God became thus the constant habit of his mind, so that when seemingly immersed in the tumult of secular affairs he could without break or effort pass on at once and enter face to face with the Divine Presence.

One result of the lack of interest in Dunstan's monastic career was the rapid dismissal by Bishop Stubbs of the problem of the date of his birth as 'not in itself of great importance'.[1]   As a matter of fact his acceptance of the year 925 reduced the chronology of Dunstan's life to absurdity, and led to the rejection of some historical statements which are as well founded as any of the period. For we must needs deny that Athelstan was crowned by Archbishop Athelm: we must suppose that Dunstan was ordained priest before he was fourteen, and became an abbot at eighteen or twenty: or, as an alternative, we must distrust the only records that describe his career.   I have dealt with the question fully elsewhere,[2] and will here only say that the trouble has arisen from the post-Conquest interpretation of the vague words of his earliest biographer, who says that 'in the times of the rule of K. Athelstan there arose', or 'was born' (*oritur*), 'a strenuous youth in the country of the West-Saxons'.[3]   On the strength of this passage Osbern of Canterbury fixed Dunstan's birth in 925, which was the first year, according to the altered annal of the Parker Chronicle, of K. Athelstan's reign.

It is interesting to note an isolated voice of protest in a mediæval chronicler whose work is

[1] *Mem. of St Dunstan*, p. lxxiv.
[2] *The Saxon Bishops of Wells*, pp. 28 ff.
[3] *Ibid.*, p. 6.

practically unknown. In 1691 Gale printed considerable extracts from a MS of John of Wallingford, a monk of St Albans who was the contemporary of Matthew Paris. In a passage which Gale did not print there occurs this notice of St Dunstan's birth: 'He was born therefore in the time of Athelstan, not when he was reigning, but when he was governing the kingdom under the sceptre of his father. If any one prefers to believe what is commonly reported and written on this subject, let him reckon up the sequence of events, and he will find St Dunstan to have presided over the abbey of Glastonbury when he was but twenty years of age or very little more. But on this question, since it is of no profit, we do not propose to tug the rope of controversy (*sed super hoc, quia inutile est, non multum trahimus ex alterutraque parte funem*).[1] If Gale had printed this passage, it is possible that John of Wallingford's protest might have had some result. We cannot indeed accept his ingenious solution of the difficulty. We must either interpret *oritur* as referring to Dunstan's first appearance as a youth of promise, or suppose that his anonymous biographer had nothing to guide him as to the exact date of Athelstan's accession.

If we suppose Dunstan to have been born in 909, our chronological difficulties disappear. We get back 923 as the date of Plegmund's death and Athelm's translation to Canterbury, instead of 914

---

[1] Cotton MS *Julius* D 7. I have printed extracts from it in *Som. Arch. Soc. Proceedings*, LXII (1916), pp. 1–25, 'Memories of St Dunstan in Somerset'.

as recent historians have given it: Athelm's death
and Wulfhelm's accession will fall in 926: Dunstan's ordination as priest may be assigned to 939,
when he had reached the canonical age of thirty;
and his appointment to the abbey of Glastonbury
will not have taken place until he was thirty-four
or thirty-five.

I should wish here to cite—with some necessary
modification of minor details—a passage from
a letter of the late Edmund Bishop [1] to whose
learning and counsel I am under a peculiar
obligation. It is, as he says, a mere flight of the
imagination based on the recovered facts as to the
succession of the Wells bishops and the date of
St Dunstan's birth: but to me it has been a welcome aid, as his conversational letters so often
were, in the endeavour to piece together and
understand the fragmentary items out of which
our tenth century history has to be built up.

It is certainly—on the face of things—a very notable
circumstance that from this very unsettled and hitherto
unorganized Christianity—Somersetshire—so soon as any
sort of ecclesiastical order is established with the foundation of the sees of Ramsbury, Wells, Crediton—the first
two Wells bishops (excuse my saying so: a trumpery
settlement, in a hollow out in the wilds—just look at the
hills about you) should go straight to the chair of Canterbury. And the first is in some way related to Ælfheah
who becomes bishop of Winchester—if the relationship
be only that of cousins 'removed'. Moreover it is a family
business: Athelm a brother of Dunstan's father, Ælfheah
a relative of Dunstan; both of them, each in his own
generation, concerned for this 'hope of the house'. And

------

[1] Dated 6 Feb. 1914.

in addition to this, at least through the lady Ethelfreda (an unattached widow much mixed up with the royal house)[1], connected by some sort of relationship, however remote, with the kingly line. Then we must not forget Kensige the bishop of Lichfield, who if a relative of Dunstan is so of Ælfheah too: and, as Stubbs pointed out in the record of Bishop Coenwald's visit to St Gall, 'Keondrud', who is admitted to the fraternity of St Gall on that occasion, would seem to be St Dunstan's mother.

It is a perfect network. Just this one family: and holding close together. But for the sudden emergence of this family there must be reason somewhere. If Athelm be the brother of Heorstan and St Dunstan's birth be somewhere say about 909 or 910, it takes us back even by an estimated age of these two brothers (and they must have had a father and mother before them) to the days when Alfred in dire straits was making a stand in remote Somerset against the Danes . . . And then thinking, imagining, dreaming so, one begins to feel one understands why that story of the death of St Edmund the king at the hand of the pagan Danes affected Dunstan so to the end of his days. How it must have recalled to him incidents that he had heard in his childhood of the successful stand against those heathen hordes, in that far West Country—Somerset—that native land to which there is enough to show, I think, in the account of his later years, he remained faithfully attached.

They must have been a capable, a 'strong minded' (remember Kensige of Lichfield was with Dunstan in remonstrating with Edwy on his coronation day), but also a 'having' race.

Yes: with names and dates once fixed, all the earlier life will come clear, will be a natural story. We shall no longer have to put up with the very funny story of the precocious young gentleman of fifteen who was crazy to

[1] 'Haec igitur omne semen regium, de quo ipsa nobilitatis originem duxit, intimo caritatis ardore dilexit.'

G

marry, and the bishop of the capital city as a remedy seizing on the young person and off-hand ordaining him priest, &c. &c. . . .

Another point on which I have diverged from the modern tradition concerns the supposed foreign origin of the monastic revival in England. It is the way of reformers, and yet more of their immediate successors, to exaggerate the evil conditions which have called for amendment: and there are passages in late tenth-century writers which speak as if monasticism had entirely died out in England. Dunstan's earliest biographer actually called him the first abbot of the English race. But the facts are against this view. William of Malmesbury wrote his book *On the Antiquity of the Church of Glastonbury* with the express purpose of proving from extant records that there had been many abbots at Glastonbury before St Dunstan. That Dunstan's monasticism was in any sense a foreign importation never occurred to him: he knew how Dunstan had come to be a monk, and he knew that under him as abbot the Benedictine Rule was well observed at Glastonbury in K. Edmund's days. It is true that the reform movements in France and Flanders preceded the English movement by a full generation, and that the intercourse between England and the Continent in K. Athelstan's reign was such that the good fame of these reforms must have cheered the hearts of men of religion who mourned over the decay of monastic life at home. But our records do not warrant us in saying more than this.

We shall return presently to the subject of these foreign movements. Meanwhile we may conveniently consider at this point an ancient calendar of the church of Glastonbury, which will throw a little light on the obscure question of the traditions of the abbey in St Dunstan's time.

Among the noteworthy consequences of the growing intercourse of England with the Continent which marked the reign of Athelstan was the introduction of the Caroline minuscule writing. Before the end of the tenth century it had, at any rate for certain specially magnificent books, not merely modified but even supplanted the native hand. Sir E. M. Thompson has noted slight indications of the influence of this foreign hand as early as a carefully written charter of K. Athelstan in 931.[1] As the revived English monasticism came in contact with the great continental abbeys, it was natural that the progress of this change in handwriting should be hastened. The literary movement under Ethelwold at Winchester gave a special opportunity for the introduction of the new style. The splendid Benedictional which was written for the bishop himself is not the only Winchester book which illustrates this.[2] But, if

[1] *Greek and Latin Paleography* (1893), p. 251. (The charter is B.C.S. 677).

[2] *Ibid.*, p. 253. Similarly from Ramsey probably came the Sacramentary of Winchelcombe' (Orleans, 105: described by Delisle, *Anc. Sacr.*, p. 211). It is of the end of the tenth century, and belonged to a church of St Peter and St Kenelm; and it was given to St Benedict (Fleury): '[patro]no suo Benedicto ob sui memoriam a transmarinis partibus misit ...' Unfortunately the donor's name is lost. Winchelcombe had

England was ready to welcome the good gifts that came from abroad, yet in this as in other matters there is no servile copying. 'It is interesting to notice,' says Sir E. M. Thompson in reference to this Benedictional, 'that, while the letters are of the foreign type, there is a strongly marked English character in the writing which is unmistakable, even if it were not known that the scribe was an Englishman.' [1] 'The character', he says, 'which the English scribes impressed upon this foreign style is that of roundness'; and this, he has already shown, was an inheritance from the Irish hand out of which their own was developed.

If St Ethelwold's Benedictional, a splendid monument of English art, adorned with pictures and gleaming with gold, is characteristic of the prelate who caused it to be made, yet it cannot compete in historical importance with the newly recovered Bosworth Psalter, which was almost certainly written for St Dunstan's use at Canterbury. Here again there is high art, but under severe restraint: there are no pictures, and the great capitals present a subdued harmony of many colours, but no gold. The suggestion is not

Germanus as its first abbot under St Oswald; when the persecution came he went back to Fleury and stayed there three years; he was afterwards abbot of Ramsey (see below, p. 131). The writing is of the same character as the Ethelwold and Robert Benedictionals, and a Fleury Benedictional (B.N. lat. 987) sent from Ramsey to Abbot Gauzlin (c. 1010 or 1020): see *Vita Gauzlini* § 43 in *Neues Archiv* III 369 (first ed. by Delisle in 1853, *Mém. de la Soc. archéologique de l'Orléanais*, t. II).

[1] *Ibid.*, p. 267.

fanciful that here as there the character of the man stands revealed.

The version of the Psalms is that which is known as the Roman in contrast to the Gallican, which latter did not find acceptance in England until the Norman Conquest. St Benedict's division of the Psalter is marked throughout, showing that the book was written for a monastic and not for a secular church; and a hymnary is added, containing a hundred hymns for use in the Divine Office. Minor additions complete the book for the recitation of the Office according to St Benedict's Rule, and its worn corners testify to a diligent use in choir.

To this remarkable book a calendar is prefixed on two folios of a somewhat finer vellum, written later, but, as it would seem, at no great distance of date. We find here St Dunstan's feast which began to be celebrated almost immediately after his death in 988; but not that of St Alphege, who was martyred in 1012, and whose body was translated from London to Canterbury in 1023. A comparison of this calendar with that of the Leofric Missal proves that both are derived from a calendar of St Dunstan's own abbey of Glastonbury; but the writer of the Bosworth copy has adapted it by some additions and omissions to the needs of Canterbury. In the hands of that master of liturgical and historical detail, Edmund Bishop, this calendar has proved to be the key to the whole problem of the development of English mediæval calendars. His elaborate Introduction cannot safely be neglected by the student of the religious life of England from the tenth to the twelfth century. Calendars might be thought as remote from the interests of the modern historian as lists of relics; but they reflect the changing times, and may throw curious side-lights on the characters of the men who brought about the changes.

The calendar of Glastonbury, now that we can reconstruct it for the great days of Dunstan's rule, has a quite exceptional interest. When we have rescued William of Malmesbury's work on *The Antiquity of the Church of Glastonbury* from the confusion brought about by successive additions and interpolations,[1] we desire to know, if it be at all possible, how far back beyond the historian's own days those traditions go which he on careful inquiry was minded to accept as genuine. Let us note then some of the saints of the British Isles who are named in this old Glastonbury calendar.

First the Irish saints:

> St Patrick senior in Glaston.
> St Patrick bishop.
> St Bridget.

St Patrick does not surprise us: for we know that in Dunstan's boyhood Irish pilgrims came to visit his tomb—though some men said it was not his, but the tomb of a later namesake.[2] Our

---

[1] See *Somerset Historical Essays*, pp. 1–25.

[2] *Memorials*, p. 10 (cf. p. lxxviii, n.). The Arras MS has 'beati Patricii junioris', and this is printed by Stubbs. The Cotton and St Gall MSS read 'senioris', and it would seem that this was read by Osbern and William of Malmesbury (*ibid.*, pp. 75 and 257).

calendar allows for both. Again, William of Malmesbury says that it was not thought certain that St Bridget lay at Glastonbury, though she had left memorials there of her stay. The chapel of St Mary Magdalene in what was (and still is) called Beckery, or Little Ireland, came to be known as St Bridget's chapel. These traditions, then, were already current in the tenth century.

Two other entries occur with the addition of the words 'in Glaston'. These are St Aidan the bishop and St Ceolfrid the abbot. The latter was the great abbot of Jarrow and Wearmouth, for whom the famous *Codex Amiatinus* of the Vulgate was written. How came Glastonbury to make the audacious claim that these saints from the far north rested in her burial-ground ? We turn again to William of Malmesbury. 'When the Danes,' he says, 'were ravaging Northumbria, a certain abbot Tica took refuge at Glastonbury, and was made abbot there in 754. He brought with him relics of St Aidan and the bodies of Ceolfrid, Benedict (Biscop) and other abbots of Wearmouth: also of Bede the Presbyter and Abbess Hilda.' Another tradition said that these saints were sent to Glastonbury by K. Edmund, when on his northern expedition. This was of course when Dunstan was the abbot. William of Malmesbury in his various writings wavers between these two explanations, but he seems to have decided ultimately for the earlier date.[1] Our calendar tells us at any rate that in St Dunstan's time Aidan and Ceolfrid were certainly believed to

[1] *Som. Hist. Essays*, pp. 19 f.

lie at Glastonbury. For St Aidan we can cite two
other early authorities. The first is the English
tract on the Resting-places of the Saints, which
Liebermann published in 1889. This collection,
he tells us, was begun before 995 and completed
between 1013 and 1030. Here we read: 'There
rest in Glastonbury St Aidan and St Patrick and
many other saints.' [1] The second witness is the
O. E. Martyrology, of which we have one small
fragment that goes back to *c.* 850. Of the two
full copies one was written in the first half, the
other in the second half, of the tenth century.[2]
The earlier copy says of St Aidan: 'His bones
are half of them in Scotland (*on Scottum*), half in
St Cuthbert's Minster.'   But the later copy has
for the second part of the sentence: 'half at
Glastonbury in St Mary's minster'.   The alteration
would be in harmony with the tradition that
'relics of St Aidan' (not the whole body, be it
noted) came south as late as K. Edmund's time:
but it is quite possible that a Glastonbury monk,
in making the correction, wished to assert a very
ancient claim of his abbey.   We are not here
concerned with the truth of the tradition, but with
the early date to which it can be taken back:
for myself, however, I see no reason to question the
truth of it in one or other of its forms.

We turn to our calendar again, and read the
name of 'St Gildas the Wise'.   Gildas the historian, says William of Malmesbury, spent many

---

[1] *Die Heiligen Englands*, p. 17.

[2] *Early Eng. Texts Soc.*, no. 116.   Dr. Herzfeld, the editor,
tells us that this later text is 'a West-Saxon transcript of
a Mercian MS.'

years at Glastonbury. We cannot be sure that the words which follow in the *De Antiquitate* come from William of Malmesbury himself: 'And there he died in A.D. 512, and was buried in the Old Church before the altar'.[1] We now know that at any rate he was commemorated there in St Dunstan's day.

Two other names we will pick out before we leave this calendar: St Paulinus bishop of Rochester, and St Wilfrid bishop. The commemoration of the former is fully accounted for by William of Malmesbury's record of a curious tradition: 'Paulinus, companion of St Augustine, when bishop of Rochester after having been archbishop of York, is said to have covered the wattled church with wooden planks'.[2] As this venerable church was standing when William of Malmesbury wrote, we may assume that its aspect was such as seemed to him compatible with this story. The calendar goes some way to bear out the tradition, which quite possibly was true. It is hard to see why otherwise Paulinus should have been commemorated at Glastonbury at all. As to St Wilfrid, that wandering prelate is said by his biographer to have visited K. Centwine of the West Saxons, and to have been the friend of K. Caedwalla, who made him gifts of land. A Glastonbury charter said that K. Centwine gave him Wedmore: and it was believed that the abbey had afterwards received it and lost it again.[3] Here at any rate we have an explanation of his somewhat unexpected mention in our calendar.

[1] *Som. Hist. Essays*, p. 12. [2] *Ibid.*, p. 19.
[3] *Ibid.*, p. 32.

V

ST ETHELWOLD

THE reputation of St Ethelwold suffers in the present day from the recognition now more generously accorded to his two great fellow-workers in the cause of monastic reform. St Oswald has always been regarded as the gentlest spirit of the three: his 'holy guile' which rendered violence unnecessary at Worcester delighted William of Malmesbury, and his wisdom in dealing with landed estates has been eulogized by the late Professor Maitland. St Dunstan's character has been vindicated, first by John Richard Green and then more completely by Bishop Stubbs, who in his zeal to praise the statesman minimized the archbishop's share in the promotion of monasticism. So it has come about that Ethelwold is made the scapegoat: he has to bear the burden of the unpopularity which the movement is said to have aroused: he was the harsh, unyielding, hasty reformer, who struck down all who opposed him, and whose cruelty produced a reaction the moment that he was dead.

I do not wish to deny that he was less gentle or less prudent than Oswald, or to claim for him the massiveness and calm of Dunstan. But I would point out that here as elsewhere a distinction must be drawn between pre-Conquest and post-Conquest appreciations; and I would illustrate the matter by a single contrast. The Peterborough Chronicle

(E) tells us that, in the year after he was consecrated to Winchester, Ethelwold 'drave out the clerks from the bishopric; for that they would keep no rule; and he settled there monks'. Now these words correctly represent the view of the time when they were written, namely, about the year 1121. But the Parker Chronicle (A), which is a contemporary authority, tells us under the same year, 964; 'Here King Edgar drave out the priests from (Win)chester, from the Old Minster and the New Minster, and from Chertsey and Middleton, and settled them with monks.' The difference is a striking one; and we shall do well to remember that, whereas at Worcester Oswald was at a distance from the court and could bide his time, Ethelwold at Winchester had an eager young king to deal with, whose zeal for speedy reform is well attested, and who actually sent one of his chief ministers to hasten the departure of the clerks from the cathedral church.

Our chief authority for the history of St Ethelwold is the Life written by the learned abbot Ælfric, famous for his translations and homilies in the English tongue, who was trained by the saint in the monastic life, and who wrote in Latin for the monks of the new abbey of Eynsham a simplified edition of the *Regularis Concordia*, which he tells us had been compiled by St Ethelwold himself in conjunction with the bishops and abbots of K. Edgar's time. Ælfric's style is simple and straightforward, though his Latin is bald and occasionally halting. This Life was dedicated to Kenulf, the bishop of Winchester, who succeeded St Alphege on his promotion to Canterbury in November 1005, and who held the see but for a single year. St Ethelwold had been dead, we are told, twenty years: since he died in August 984, the work may have been written in 1004 and presented to Bishop Kenulf at the end of 1005. It is therefore an historical document of the first class; but it survives in a single MS, written apparently in France in the eleventh century.[1]

It was entirely superseded by an enlargement, written in flowing Latin but containing hardly anything fresh that could claim to be of value. This enlargement is anonymous: it rewrites most of Ælfric's sentences at double or treble their length, but often retains his actual words, even where he uses the first person and speaks of what he had heard from the saint himself. William of Malmesbury, who makes use of this expanded Life, tells us that it was written by Wulfstan the precentor of Winchester. Wulfstan is mentioned in connexion with a miracle at the end of Ælfric's Life, and he is known as a versifier who wrote in praise of St Swithun and St Ethelwold at some time before the death of Archbishop Sigeric in 996. If he was the author of the amplified Life, he must have written it almost immediately after Ælfric's book came out. The reasons for the

---

[1] Paris, *Bibl. Nat.* lat. 5362. This Life was known to Mabillon in a Fécamp MS (probably the same codex), but he preferred to print the enlarged form of the Life. Ælfric's Life was first printed by Joseph Stevenson in 1858: *Hist. Abingd.* (Rolls Ser.), ii. 255 ff.

identification seem to have been two: first, that the writer uses the first person, as Ælfric does, in speaking of what had been told by the saint himself, and therefore must have been a contemporary; and, secondly, that he inserts into the Life a long passage in verse which forms part of the introduction to Wulfstan's poem on St Swithun. William of Malmesbury's view was accepted by Mabillon, and, so far as I know, it has never been challenged. But a close comparison of the two works has convinced me that this longer Life, with its studied heightening of the glory of the saint and its introduction of pious reflections after the usual manner of the hagiologist, was written at least a generation later, and indeed quite probably by a Norman monk of Winchester at the end of the eleventh century.

I will give here but two out of the many points of detail which have led me to this conclusion: the first is a point of fact, the second a point of style. The later writer states that St Ethelwold was buried in the crypt on the south side of the altar; and a blind man goes into the 'antrum sarcophagi' and stays all night. There is no hint of this in Ælfric's Life, in which the man is simply led to the saint's tomb. Now in a later part of Wulfstan's poem, which is not quoted by our author, Bishop Alphege, St Ethelwold's successor, is specially praised for having 'added the crypts', and definite mention is made of a crypt that supported the great altar. There seems to be an inconsistency here. The point of style is the systematic change of 'clerks' into 'canons'. But

the 'priests' or 'clerks' whom the monks superseded are never called 'canons' in the tenth
century, nor is that term to be found except in
some foreign context until its occurrence in the
Laws of K. Ethelred in 1008. The change however is constantly made after the Conquest, as for
example in the later forms of the Anglo-Saxon
Chronicle.[1]

I shall therefore leave out of account the later
Life, only noting as a point of interest that in the
MS of St Évroul from which Mabillon printed it
this Life is copied, according to Delisle's judgement, by the hand of the historian Orderic Vitalis,
an Englishman by birth, who was trained as a boy
in the monastery of St Évroul, of which he was
the conspicuous ornament in the first half of the
twelfth century.[2]

St Ethelwold's parents were resident at Winchester in the time of K. Edward the Elder. We
may place his birth about the same time as that
of St Dunstan. His name suggests that he may
have been of noble descent, and he found a place,
as Dunstan did, in K. Athelstan's court. The
king saw his worth and commended him to the
bishop of Winchester, Ælfheah the Bald, who
ordained both Dunstan and Ethelwold to the
priesthood on the same day. With Ælfheah he
remained until K. Athelstan's death: shortly
afterwards he went to Glastonbury where Dunstan
had been made abbot. Here the two friends lived

[1] See Additional Notes B and C.
[2] See Delisle's article on Orderic Vitalis and his handwriting in *Journal des Savants*, August 1903.

for some time together as master and pupil; and, when at last Ethelwold decided to become a monk, the new movement was fairly begun.

Of the monastic revival on the Continent we shall speak more fully later; but a few words must be said here. It may be dated from the foundation of Cluny in 910, just about the time of Dunstan's birth. Among the monasteries reformed by Odo the second abbot of Cluny (924–41) was Fleury, or St Benet's on the Loire (c. 930), which, however, after Odo's death had an abbot of its own and was not dependent on Cluny. Simultaneously a great revival was taking place in Lorraine and Flanders under Gerard of Brogne, to whom was due the reform of Blandinium, or St Peter's, at Ghent in 937, and St Bertin's abbey at St Omer in 944. These foreign movements must have been watched with interest by the younger English reformers, but they cannot be shown to have had any direct influence upon them until a later period. Indeed the only trace of contact would seem to be the curious tradition that Oda who became archbishop of Canterbury in 941 received the monastic habit from Fleury.[1] Indirectly however the continental movement seriously affected Ethelwold's career. This eager neophyte, whose training at Athelstan's court had brought him into contact with the wider civilization across the sea, was desirous of studying the new monasticism at close quarters. We do not know to what monastery his thoughts were directed: the fact that at a later time he sent one

[1] See *St Oswald and the Church of Worcester*, pp. 41 f.

of his own pupils to study at Fleury is not decisive, for Fleury had by then for several years been the home of another Englishman, Oswald. Whatever his plan may have been, it was frustrated by the prudence of the queen-mother Edith, who warned her son K. Edred not to run the risk of losing from the kingdom a man of such conspicuous gifts. At her suggestion and with Dunstan's approbation the king gave him the derelict monastery of Abingdon, the estates of which had for the most part come into the royal hands in K. Alfred's days. But forty manses remained, and some forlorn buildings which sheltered a few clerks. The king himself had sumptuous buildings there, and a hundred cassates of land; and these he was prepared to hand over, if Ethelwold would restore the monastery after the manner of Dunstan's reform of Glastonbury. Ethelwold undertook the task. Three clerks he took with him from Glastonbury—Osgar, Foldbricht, and Frithegar; with these came one from Winchester—Ordbricht; and one from London—Eadric. These men were trained by Ethelwold; presently others joined them, and Ethelwold was made their abbot. The brief list of names may detain us a moment. It cannot be mere coincidence that in the course of the next twenty or thirty years four out of the five occur among the abbots of the restored monastic houses. Osgar followed Ethelwold as abbot of Abingdon, Foldbricht is found as abbot of Pershore, Frithegar as abbot of Evesham, and Ordbricht as abbot of Chertsey: only Eadric of London eludes our attempt to trace him. This serves to show the calibre of the younger men whom Dunstan's personality had begun to attract to the monastic life.

The king was a generous benefactor, and the queen-mother more generous still. The king came to measure out the foundations of the monastic buildings with his own hand; but death had already set its mark on his frail body, and he died before the church had even been begun. K. Edred died on 23 November 955. The reign of Edwy is passed over in silence by Ethelwold's biographer. Even Mr Stenton's researches have not pierced the obscurity that shrouds Abingdon at this period, though he suggests that the gifts of K. Edred and his mother were largely withdrawn, and that the monastic life was brought to a standstill.[1] It may have been that at this juncture Ethelwold sent his leading disciple Osgar to visit Fleury, where he would have found Oswald and perhaps some others from England. We may remember that Dunstan himself was sheltering from the political storm in the abbey of St Peter at Ghent. It was time that the English movement should seek spiritual reinforcement from the older movements across the channel. From Corbey in France Ethelwold brought skilled monks to give instruction in chanting.[2] And we shall see

[1] F. M. Stenton, *Early History of Abingdon*, p. 49.

[2] The Lambeth MS of Florence of Worcester has under the year 948 an account (not printed in the editions) of the monastery of Abingdon, which passes into a brief Life of Ethelwold clearly taken from the revised form of Ælfric's Life. It agrees to a large extent with passages in the *Historia*

later that in the preface to the *Regularis Concordia* both Fleury and Ghent find grateful mention.

We take up the story again with the consecration of the new church at Abingdon in K. Edgar's reign. It is dedicated, as the Old Church of Glastonbury was dedicated, to the Blessed Virgin Mary. Events meanwhile have been moving swiftly. Dunstan is now at Canterbury, 'columna immobilis,' as Ælfric's narrative calls him. Ethelwold is consecrated to Winchester in 963, and Osgar, returned from Fleury, takes his place as abbot of Abingdon—all this before the church has been dedicated. The interest now changes from Abingdon to a wider sphere.

Before we come to the fateful year 964, which the Chronicle assigns to the expulsion of the clerks from Winchester, let us recall the progress of the movement, and set down a few dates, the earlier among which can be only approximate. Dunstan becomes abbot of Glastonbury by K. Edmund's appointment *c.* 943: Ethelwold joins him, and presently becomes a monk, *c.* 946; he goes to

Abbendunensis (Claudius c 9). What the relation between these two is seems rather uncertain—they both belong to the latter part of the twelfth century: but they have one point at least in common that is not found in the revised Life of Ethelwold, which elsewhere lies behind them both. This is the statement that, when many were attracted to Abingdon from various parts of England by reason of the stricter life led there, and differed *more legendi canendique*, Ethelwold summoned skilled men from Corbey in France, then famous for its ecclesiastical discipline, in order that his monks might imitate them *in legendo psallendoque* (*Anglia Sacra*, i. 165; *Hist. Abingd.* [Rolls Ser.] I 129). The later form of the *Hist. Abingd.* (Claudius в 6) does not give this.

Abingdon *c.* 954. Edwy's accession at the end of 955 leads to the fall from power of Dunstan and the aged queen Edith. The Mercians revolt and choose Edgar as their king in 957. Dunstan then returns from his exile in Flanders, and is consecrated bishop by Archbishop Oda, being put in charge of Worcester and presently of London also. K. Edwy dies in October 959. Under Edgar the kingdoms are reunited, and Dunstan becomes archbishop in 960. Oswald, who had returned from Fleury at the moment of Archbishop Oda's death (2 June 958), succeeds Dunstan at Worcester in 961, and at once founds a small monastery at Westbury-on-Trym.

The see of Winchester had fallen on evil days since the death of Bishop Ælfheah the Bald on 2 March 951. Of his successor Ælfsige no good is recorded: his translation to Canterbury in 959 was quickly followed by his death in crossing the Alps on the way to Rome. Winchester was given to a Brihthelm whose identity is somewhat uncertain. The irregularities of the clerks of the cathedral church are the less surprising, if the bishop's seat had been unworthily filled for more than ten years. The political troubles were a further cause of moral and spiritual decline: these 'nobiles clerici', as they are called in the Hyde *Liber Vitae*, were probably for the most part of Edwy's party, and little disposed to submit to Edgar's more rigorous rule.

It is, as we have said, to K. Edgar that according to the A.-S. Chronicle the expulsion of the clerks was due. This is borne out by the testimony of the *Liber Vitae* of Hyde, in a prefatory passage which was probably written before 990. Ælfric however in his Life of Ethelwold ascribes the expulsion to the bishop himself. He adds, indeed, that the king's leave had been granted, and that the king's minister Wulfstan (i. e. Wulfstan of Dalham) was sent to hasten the matter and to give the clerks the alternative of retiring or taking the monastic habit. Ælfric belonged to a younger generation and was recording an event which had happened forty years before. It may have seemed to the honour of the saint that his part in so great a reform should receive the fullest emphasis. Ælfric's account was probably known to the anonymous writer of St Oswald's Life.[1] It was repeated in the enlarged Life of St Ethelwold, and gave the cue to subsequent writers.

We cannot acquit Ethelwold of responsibility for what appears to us high-handed action. But we must do him justice, and we may fairly plead that if the zeal which planned the change was his, the violence with which it was carried out was the king's. And we may add that outside Winchester no similar act of violence is on record in connexion with Ethelwold's reforms.

Here then is the story as Ælfric records it[2]:

There were at that time in the Old Minster, where was the bishop's seat, evil-mannered clerks (*malemorigerati clerici*), lofty, insolent and luxurious, so much so that some of them disdained to celebrate their masses in their

---

[1] *Historians of York* (R.S.), i. 427.
[2] *Hist. Abingd.*, ii. 260.

turns; repudiating wives whom they had married when they should not, and then taking yet others; and even given up to gluttony and drunkenness. This could the holy Ethelwold ill endure, and having received licence of K. Edgar he expelled full speedily from the minster these criminous blasphemers of God; and bringing monks from Abingdon he settled them there, being at once their abbot and their bishop. Now so it was that, when the monks who came from Abingdon were standing at the entrance of the church, the clerks within were ending the mass, singing for the Communion: 'Serve the Lord with fear, and rejoice unto Him with trembling: get you discipline (*apprehendite disciplinam*), lest ye perish from the right way'. It was as though they said: 'We are not willing to serve the Lord, nor to keep His discipline: but do ye so, lest ye perish even as we.' And the monks when they heard their chant said the one to the other: 'Why tarry we without? Lo, we are called to enter in.'

The words from the second Psalm are appointed, as the author of the enlarged Life noted, for the service of the first Saturday in Lent. The coincidence may well have removed the last scruple of the most conscientious of the intruders. Ælfric goes on:

Moreover the king sent one of the most noble of his ministers, Wulfstan by name, along with the bishop; and he by the royal authority commanded the clerks with all speed to give place to the monks, or else to receive the monastic habit. But they in hatred of the monastic life thereupon departed from the church: yet afterwards three of them were converted to the life according to the Rule, to wit, Eadsin, Wulfsin and Wilstan. Now up till then there were no monks among the English people, save only in Glastonbury and Abingdon.

These last words must not be pressed too

closely. Oswald was back from Fleury, and had begun his settlement at Westbury; and it is impossible not to think that there were monks at Canterbury—even if not at Christ Church, yet certainly at St Augustine's abbey. Once again we must remember that the writer belongs to the generation after the period of the great reform.

The expulsion of clerks from the New Minster soon followed, and the monks there introduced were placed under the rule of Ethelgar, who had been trained by Dunstan at Glastonbury,[1] and was destined to succeed him at Canterbury. About the same time Ethelwold appointed Etheldrida to rule the Nunnaminster at Winchester.

St Ethelwold's activities now took a wider range. Ely, Peterborough, and Thorney all came under his care; for the reform was moving apace. 'So it was', says his biographer, 'that with the king's consent, by the counsel and action partly of Dunstan and partly of Ethelwold, monasteries were established everywhere in England, for monks and for nuns, under abbots and abbesses living according to rule.'[2]   We note here the part duly assigned to Archbishop Dunstan, who must by this time have had Westminster, Bath, and Malmesbury in hand. We pass on to speak of Bishop Ethelwold's three restorations, taking them in reverse order.

Thorney is but seven miles from Peterborough. K. Edgar's foundation charter is a document of questionable authenticity, which has points of

---

[1] *De Antiq. Glaston.* in Hearne's *Ad. of Domerham*, i. 92.
[2] *Hist. Abingd.*, ii. 262.

contact with the preface to the *Regularis Concordia*: it tells the legendary story of the place, and gives a list of properties; it states that the new church was built 'to the praise of the Trinity', and had an altar of the B.V.M. at the east, one of St Peter for the people in the nave, and one of St Benedict in a northern apse.[1] The first abbot was Godeman, who has been identified with the writer of Ethelwold's splendid Benedictional.[2]

The early story of Peterborough, or Medeshamsted as it was called until the *burh* was built after the refoundation, is a mass of legend. Even Ethelwold's labours have not escaped an embroidery of fiction. But the main facts are clearly stated by Ælfric. Ethelwold acquired the site by purchase from the king and the nobles of the land, and having planted monks there placed over them as abbot Aldulf, who afterwards followed Oswald as archbishop of York and bishop of Worcester.

The story is borne out by a series of Anglo-Saxon documents, happily preserved to us in a Peterborough register in the possession of the Society of Antiquaries.[3] Here we have a record of Ethelwold's gifts to the new abbey. First comes a list of church ornaments, a Gospel Book, crosses, candle-sticks, bells, vestments, and so forth: then a list of twenty-one books, including works of Bede, St Augustine, Isidore, &c., the last two being of special interest, 'De litteris grecorum' and 'Liber bestiarum': finally, there

[1] B.C.S. 1297: cf. 1131.
[2] He is entered in the *Liber Vitae* of New Minster, p. 24.
[3] Printed in B.C.S. 1128–31.

is a record of the estates which he gave. Further documents enter into particulars as to these and other estates, illustrating the generosity and the businesslike methods of Abbot Aldulf as well as of the bishop himself. One estate the bishop acquired by exchange with a certain Wulfstan who had come by it in a way which illustrates the manners of the time. A widow and her son had practised pin-sticking witchcraft on Ælsi, Wulfstan's father. The widow was taken and drowned at London Bridge; her son became an outlaw: their land was given by K. Edgar, to whom it was forfeit, to Ælsi and his son Wulfstan, who presently gave it by exchange to Bishop Ethelwold.

Of the energetic Abbot Aldulf William of Malmesbury tells us that after he had become archbishop of York he emulated Oswald's generosity in his gifts to the abbey of Fleury, where he had a great name for the abundance of his presents. This is but one of many examples of the gratitude which English monasticism continued to show to this famous foreign house.[1]

We come lastly to Ely, of which Ælfric tells us that

It was ennobled by the relics and miracles of St Etheldreda the virgin and her sisters, but was at that time derelict and given over to the royal purse. Ethelwold bought it from the king, and established there many monks, setting over them as father his disciple Brihtnoth : he enriched it abundantly with buildings and with lands.

On 9 May 957 K. Edwy had granted to Arch-

[1] See above, p. 97.

bishop Oda 40 manses 'æt Helig'. The original charter was edited by Napier and Stevenson (*Crawford Charters*, no. V). The editors say that Ely 'cannot be the subject of the present grant, since the whole of the Isle of Ely was then in possession of St Æðelþryð's monastery'; but they do not suggest any satisfactory alternative. We should gather however from Ælfric's statement and also from the *Liber Eliensis* that the monastery was in the king's hands and the lands to a great extent at his disposal. We are in fact told that about the year 970 Bishop Ethelwold bought 20 hides which the king had *infra insulam*.[1] By that time Oda was dead and we do not know what was the fate of the lands granted to him by K. Edwy. But we do find that a certain Thurstan, described as a Dane, was vying with Sygedwold, a bishop '*natione Graecus*', for a grant of the site of the monastery from K. Edgar. The king, however, entrusted the abbey to St Ethelwold, giving him certain lands and selling him others. It is just possible that Thurstan the Dane may have derived his interest in Ely from Archbishop Oda. It is also conceivable that Oda had cherished an intention of refounding the monastery itself on the reformed lines. Oswald his nephew was then at Fleury, and soon after the date of this charter the archbishop was urging him to return to England. When he did return it was to find that the archbishop was dead. We may further note that Ely was one of the three sites which K. Edgar is said to have offered to Oswald, just

---

[1] *Lib. Eliens.* (ed. D. J. Stewart), p. 109.

before his acceptance of Ramsey from Duke Ethelwin.[1]

To read the *Liber Eliensis* is to obtain an amazing picture of the activities of St Ethelwold. We might imagine that he had nothing else to do between the year 970 and his death in 984, but to watch over the territorial interests of this new foundation. Ely would seem to have been to him what Ramsey was to St Oswald. The two foundations were but 17 miles apart, and we need not be surprised to find that their interests sometimes clashed. Duke Brihtnoth was the hero-patron of the one, as Duke Ethelwin was of the other. Duke Ethelwin appears often in the *Liber Eliensis*, þut the monks thought him sadly biased in favour of Ramsey, and complained that they could not always get justice from him.

The gifts which St Ethelwold bestowed on Ely and other monasteries suggest that he must have had large private wealth: the lands which he gave, at any rate, cannot have come out of the see of Winchester. It is specially interesting therefore to note that the 60 hides at Harting in Sussex, which in consolidating the properties near the Isle of Ely he gave in exchange to K. Edgar, are said to have come to him 'by gift of his lord K. Athelstan': the tradition at any rate reminds us of his youthful days in the great king's court.[2]

---

[1] *Historians of York*, i. 427.

[2] *Lib. Eliens.*, p. 109: here 'Herlingeham' is printed by Stewart, but Gale's MS has 'Eartingan'. In the charters (B. C. S. 1265–7) we have 'Heartingas', but there is no reference to a gift from K. Athelstan.

Wulfstan of Dalham (near Newmarket) appears a good deal in these pages, and always as a friend of Ely. It was he who interposed when Bishop Sygedwold the Greek and Thurstan the Dane were each of them endeavouring to get K. Edgar to sell the old site of the monastery. He is described as being *a secretis* of the king, and as advising him to refound the abbey. We are told that still earlier he had held a plea at Ely, at the door of the minster, and had awarded to St Etheldreda land at Stanie: this helps to explain his interest in the site. We may remember that it was Wulfstan of Dalham whom the king sent to enforce his will upon the clerks at Winchester.[1]

In addition to his compilation of the great code of Customs known as the *Regularis Concordia,* St Ethelwold is credited with having translated the *Rule of St Benedict* into English for the sake of those who could not readily understand Latin. The *Liber Eliensis* (p. 153) informs us that K. Edgar and Ælfthryth his queen gave to St Ethelwold the manor called Suthburn (Sudbourne, co. Sussex [2]) and the charter thereto belonging—which the Count Scule had formerly possessed—on this condition, that he should translate the Rule of St Benedict from Latin into the English tongue: which accordingly he did. St Ethelwold gave Sudbourne to the abbey of Ely. It was agreed however that Duke Ethelwin, the founder of

---

[1] Ælfric's Life of Ethelwold, p. 260: in our only MS we find but the name 'Uulstanum', but we may safely restore 'æt Delham' from the revised Life.

[2] 'Sudburnham', *Domesd. Surv.* ii. 384.

Ramsey, should have a lease of this manor and also of Stoke, which the king and queen conjointly gave to Ely. Duke Ethelwin, we may observe, was brother of Duke Ethelwold who had been the queen's first husband: so that it is likely that these properties were the queen's, and that she was primarily concerned in their gift.

According to the preface to the *Regularis Concordia* Q. Ælfthryth was made responsible for all the English convents for women: and we might reasonably suppose that it was for these foundations that a translation of the Rule was specially desired. Now Dr Schröer, who has edited this translation and discussed the variant forms in which it is preserved to us, has declared that they are all derived from an original copy intended for a convent of women.[1] The proof of this he finds in the frequent appearance in them of feminine pronouns, which have been but imperfectly eliminated in the copies intended for men.

In his genealogical table of the MSS, however, Dr Schröer begins with a presumed lost original drawn up for men—the work of St Ethelwold himself: from this he derives the copy modified for the use of women, which is the source of all extant copies.[2] It would be simpler to suppose that the translation was made in the first instance for women at the special request of the queen, and that our other copies are more or less intelligent attempts to adapt it for use in monasteries of men. I throw out the suggestion in the hope that it may be thought worthy of attention.

[1] *Die angelsächsischen Prosabearbeitungen der Benedictinerregel* (1888), pp. xxviii ff.　　　　[2] *Ibid.*, p. xxxiv.

VI

ST OSWALD

OF the three great churchmen of K. Edgar's reign St Oswald has always seemed to offer the most winning personality. It may be that our estimate is derived from the post-Conquest writers who have coloured the history of the time so as to leave this impression, and still more from later controversialists who spared Oswald when they denounced the monkery of Dunstan and Ethelwold. However this may be, Oswald's career sets him somewhat apart. Like St Dunstan, indeed, he was the nephew of an archbishop of Canterbury: but unlike him and Ethelwold he was not brought up at the royal court. His uncle, Archbishop Oda, was a Dane, or at least of Danish descent on the father's side. This foreign strain in his blood may have been in part responsible for Oswald's having been the first of the three reformers to come into personal contact with the revived monasticism abroad; and it may be no mere coincidence that he was made archbishop of Danish York in succession to Oskytel, another of his kinsmen.

I have dealt so fully elsewhere with Oswald and his uncle Oda,[1] that I shall here only sketch his life and work, so as to bring out a side of the monastic movement which was largely independent

---

[1] *St Oswald and the Church of Worcester :* for Oda, pp. 38 ff.

in its origin and progress, and was not the direct outcome of Dunstan's work at Glastonbury.

When St Wulfstan, the rebuilder of the church of Worcester in the Norman days, saw the destruction of St Oswald's church, he wept tears of regret for that ancient relic of the past. Oswald himself had saved the old church of St Peter, and had built his new church of St Mary by its side. It was the very greatness of St Oswald's 'basilica', as it was called, which made it necessary to take it down, so as to clear the site for one that was greater still. The little church of St Peter had survived because it was too small to be in the way in those less crowded days when space was readily available.

That little church of St Peter, where the bishop's stool had been set since the days of the first bishop, Bosel, has a pathos and a message of its own. It stands for the simple ideas of worship, ritual and architecture which were the outcome of that Irish Christianity, vivid with spiritual imagination, but innocent of pomp and circumstance, which reached Mercia from the north, mediated by the great mother Hilda, out of whose monastic schools came not less than five bishops of the seventh century, when bishops as yet were few.

These northern churchmen might be convinced by their travelled brethren that the customs of a larger Christendom could not wisely be opposed. They might accept another date for Easter, and accommodate their tonsure for the sake of unity and peace. But they were the spiritual heirs of missionaries who preached in fields or at street corners, of bishops who walked and would not ride, who practised apostolic poverty, and whose churches were hardly less humble than their dwellings.

Only the men who had seen Rome and had been inspired by Christian art, and had learned the practical gain of embodying great ideas in impressive forms—men like Benedict Biscop of Wearmouth and Wilfrid of York—were otherwise minded. Such men strove to raise the English Church from its outward meanness and to clothe it with a dignity which should compel the veneration of a people who were moving towards a higher civilization. The future was theirs; but as yet they were few. The churches which expressed their aspirations could well nigh be counted on the fingers of one hand—York, for example, and Ripon and Hexham, and the churches on the Wear, in one of which Bede was then a choir-boy. It was a movement far in advance of its times; and for centuries it seemed to stand still. Yet the old order was proving itself insufficient, and when the Danes ravaged the land its weakness was but too plain, and religion and learning alike were drowned in the flood. A few favoured spots seem to have stood out and escaped the overthrow; and from Worcester, as we have said, Alfred could still draw scholars, such as Werfrith and Plegmund and one or two more, who had books preserved out of the universal spoliation, and could read and write their Latin, and help him to turn it into English for his Wessex folk.

But, if learning survived in these remoter parts,

little had been done for the extension of religion, or for the manifestation of its power to build up institutions symbolical of its lofty truths. Monasticism, which had been powerful elsewhere, had no representation here, if I judge the evidence aright. The church of St Peter may have been re-built more than once since the earliest days, but it was insignificant still; and the community which served it—the bishop's 'family' as they were called—was declining in effectiveness as the years passed by.

Under Bishop Denebert, in 800, we find that it numbered 9 priests, 4 deacons, and 5 other persons, making 18 in all; but when St Oswald became bishop, in 961, out of 17 members of the family the priests were but two, with one deacon to serve them, and the rest were clerks who shared in the revenues of the church without contributing much, we may fear, to its spiritual effectiveness.

Worcester was but typical in this respect; for everywhere we are told the minsters were in the hands of clerks, who lived but laxly and neglected the service of God. The complaints come to us indeed from the next generation, when letters had revived and books were written once more; they came from the men who had taken the places of the defaulters and were filled with a new zeal, and who looked back on the past as a period of unrelieved darkness. But we need not deny that a change was imperatively needed if the English Church was to keep pace with the forward march of the English people.

With the tenth century Alfred's work began to bear its fruit. In the spacious days of K. Athelstan, England came in touch with the larger civilization of the Continent. There was a consciousness of growing greatness, which increased under Edmund the Magnificent and reached its climax under Edgar the Peaceable. The Church awoke to new activity as the nation throbbed with fresh life. It is commonly supposed that the revival of religion came to us from abroad. It is true that at a later stage it owed much to the experience gained by the somewhat earlier revivals in Flanders and in France; but at the outset it was, as we have already said more than once, a native movement, the outcome of the piety of men like St Ælfheah of Winchester, a monk who had carried on the true tradition of the past, and who in turn made Dunstan a monk, and inspired him in the quiet years of his work at Glastonbury, before ever his exile brought him into contact with the reformed monasticism of Ghent. From Glastonbury, untouched by foreign influences, came Ethelwold and other abbots of Dunstan's school, whose pious labours made it possible for England to receive and digest and anglicize whatever of good custom she might presently find in the reformed houses of the Continent.

We first hear of Oswald as a brilliant and attractive youth, destined for high preferment. His uncle Oda supplied him with the means to purchase the headship of a monastery at Winchester—that is to say, some church with a small community of clerks attached to it, such as in those days often passed by inheritance, in a way that Bede had denounced long before, and that was considered scandalous in the next generation. Oswald found his clerks luxurious, if not licentious, and irreformable. 'He lived like Lot in Sodom' says his biographer. It is the harsh verdict of the new age, after the reform had brought a severer standard. Oswald, at any rate, was driven to despair, and begged his uncle Oda to let him go abroad and dedicate his life in a foreign monastery. Had he been a Wessex man he would have found what he sought under Abbot Dunstan at home. But there was another strain in his blood, and the archbishop himself had, it is said, received the monastic habit from the reformed monastery of Fleury. So to Fleury Oswald went, lost as it would seem to the English Church. But Oda, in his last days, sent for him to return. He obeyed, but before he reached Canterbury the old archbishop had passed away, and Oswald went to his kinsman Oskytel at York. Then Dunstan, newly raised to Canterbury, discovered him, and with the young king Edgar's full approval chose him to take his place at Worcester.

At once he gained the hearts of all, from the dukes to the peasants: holy, humble, just, and hospitable. His little church of St Peter could not contain the multitudes who sought to hear him, and he preached in the cemetery outside, standing on the steps of the cross. His minster, or monastery, for so it was called, though it never had been served by monks, was probably in not much better case than the church he had tried to

reform at Winchester. His earliest charters show
us, as we have said, only two priests. But the
years had brought him wisdom. As soon as he
was settled in and was gaining ground, he sent
for Germanus, an Englishman who had followed
him to Fleury, and bade him instruct the priests
and others whom his piety had begun to attract.
Instead of disturbing Worcester, he planted them
at Westbury-on-Trym, forming a small monastery
with a school of boys. After four years or more,
a chance meeting with a nobleman at K. Edgar's
court opened the prospect of a really great foundation on the reformed lines.

The nobleman was a son of Duke Athelstan, 'the
Half-king,' as he was called for his semi-royal
influence, who himself in his old age became a
monk at Glastonbury. Ethelwin his eldest son
was a man of equal piety, and he offered to build
a monastery at Ramsey for Oswald's monks.
To Ramsey presently went Wynsige, a priest who
had served St Helen's, as vicar for the mother
church at Worcester; and after he had been duly
trained Oswald brought him back with several
monks of the Ramsey choir, to preside over the
'family' at Worcester and inaugurate a new
régime. We cannot fix the date when monks first
came to Worcester. We can be sure they were
there in 977, sixteen years after Oswald's consecration, and they may have come some four or
five years sooner; but time must be allowed for
the experiment at Westbury, for the foundation
of Ramsey, and for the years of Wynsige's training
there. One thing is plain. Oswald moved slowly

where resistance might be expected. He would make no sudden breach with the past. The witnesses to his charters show that there was no break in the continuity of the 'family' at St Peter's. The number of priests gradually increased, and the gaps which naturally occurred were filled with Oswald's new men; but there were no expulsions like those at Winchester, where the eager Ethelwold, under the stimulus of the no less eager king, displaced the reluctant clerks with the aid of the civil power. Nor is it true, as the Norman historians imagined, that Oswald founded a new 'family' in a new church to which he presently removed his episcopal chair. He built a new church indeed, the church of St Mary, side by side with the ancient church of his see; and he built it on the scale which was suggested by the great churches he had seen abroad, and which was actually demanded by the new conditions at home. But the 'family' who entered on this new inheritance was no other than the family of St Peter's, gradually renewed as time went on. It is significant of his temperate reform that he spared the old church with its memories of the past, and still spoke of it in one of his latest charters as the church of the bishop's throne. It was natural indeed that under later bishops the great 'basilica' of St Mary should succeed to the honour to which its superior merits obviously entitled it; but Oswald made no change.

There is one side of St Oswald's activities which has made his name familiar to students of the social development of English life. This is his administration of the estates of the church of Worcester, and in especial of the region which long afterwards was still known as Oswaldslaw. The whole subject has been dealt with by Professor Maitland in his 'Doomsday Book and Beyond'. It is only necessary here to observe that it is owing to St Oswald's methodical care in such temporal matters that we have been able to trace with security the progress of his reform, and to correct the errors into which the fancies of the post-Conquest writers had led our historians in the recent past. The number of charters issued by Oswald has no parallel for any other church. For the years from 962 to 969, for example, we have some thirty grants of leases, mostly for three lives; and, as these bear the names of the Worcester 'family', we can watch the gradual change in its composition. When we reach 977 we find that Wynsige, the leader of the monks brought in from Ramsey, stands in the first place; and by the time of St Oswald's death in 992 we may believe that this quiet transformation of a church of clerks into a church of monks had been fully made.

Besides his foundation of Ramsey, Oswald placed monks at Winchelcombe, sending Germanus the dean of Ramsey to be their abbot. In the troublous days after K. Edgar's death Germanus and his monks would seem to have been driven out, at any rate for a time; but the history of this period remains obscure.[1] Ramsey escaped owing

[1] According to *Hist. Rames.* (R.S.), p. 73, Germanus returned to Fleury, but after three years was recalled by

to its powerful lay patrons. It was for a time the home of the learned Abbo, who afterwards became abbot of Fleury. Among Abbo's pupils was Byrhtferth, a mathematician whose scientific knowledge was in advance of his age, and who also had a wide acquaintance with ancient classical authors. His works have been neglected in England, but there is a full, if not exhaustive, account of them in Richard Wülker's *Grundriss z. Gesch. d. angelsächsischen Litteratur* (1885). Amongst ourselves his name would hardly be known, were it not that Bishop Stubbs was at some pains to dispose of Mabillon's conjecture that Byrhtferth was the early biographer of St Dunstan, who is known to us only as 'B. presbyter'.[1]

St Oswald's share in the monastic movement was directly inspired by Fleury, and the school of learning which flourished at Ramsey received its impulse from Abbo of Fleury. St Dunstan, on the other hand, had come into touch with foreign monasticism at Ghent, when his great work at Glastonbury was already done. St Ethelwold had begun on the Glastonbury lines, but presently he introduced customs from Fleury and the liturgical

Oswald to Ramsey. From *Vit. Osw.* (*Historians of York*, ii. 468) we learn that he was staying as a guest at Ramsey shortly before St Oswald's death, when Duke Ethelwin paid his last visit there. The duke said that after his death it would be the wish of Germanus to go elsewhere [possibly back to Fleury]; but he prayed the monks, if occasion should arise to elect an abbot, that they would choose Germanus. He is entered as abbot of Ramsey in the *Liber Vitae* of New Minster (ed. Birch), p. 24. For Winchelcombe, see above, p. 97.

[1] *Memorials of St Dunstan*, pp. xix f.

chant from Corbey. The Dunstan-Ethelwold side of the movement was native and national in character, perhaps to a larger extent than the other: at any rate while Byrhtferth at Ramsey represents the new learning which Abbo the foreigner had brought over, the glory of the Winchester school at the same moment is the contribution to English literature made by the Homilies of Abbot Ælfric, the pupil of St Ethel-wold. But we must be careful not to sharpen the contrast unduly. The three leaders worked to-gether in unbroken harmony. They recognized the desirability of securing this harmony for the future, and the *Regularis Concordia* tells us in its preface that both sides made their contribution to the new English code, for among the experts who were brought in to advise were monks alike from Fleury and from Ghent.

Though Oswald, for some twenty out of his thirty years as bishop of Worcester, was the arch-bishop of York as well, and though Ramsey was the object of his constant care, he seems to have lived mostly at Worcester, and there he died and was buried. His last hours reveal to us the same holy humility and reverent devotion which charac-terized his whole career. It was the last day of February, 992. After a full Sunday's work on the day before, he had risen early, and after the morning prayers had washed the feet of the poor in the cloister, chanting as he did so the fifteen Psalms of Degrees, the short psalms which follow the 119th. At the end the brethren solemnly sang the words, 'The Lord which made heaven and earth give thee blessing out of Sion.' The old man knelt with the rest for the *Gloria*, but he could not rise again; and with the words of praise on his lips he passed away.

It is desirable at this point to look abroad and trace the main features of those foreign reforms, which have of necessity been so frequently mentioned already. In the year 909, to which we have assigned St Dunstan's birth, a council was held at Trosli, near Soissons, under Heriveus, the archbishop of Rheims. In the record of its acts a dark picture is drawn of the utter ruin of monasticism, which was due partly to the pagan ravages and partly to the intrusion of lay abbots with wives and children. All that the bishops are able to suggest by way of remedy is the appointment of regular abbots.[1] In the very next year (910) came the foundation of Cluny in the diocese of Mâcon. Berno, its first abbot, had already founded two small monasteries in the same part of Burgundy, at Gigny and at Beaume. At Beaume he had imposed a stringent discipline on the lines laid down by the great reformer Benedict of Aniane a hundred years before. But he had to face a strenuous and persistent opposition on the part of the younger monks: indeed by their evil report of his severity they sought to dissuade a notable recruit from joining their house. This was the great St Odo, who came to Beaume a year before Cluny was founded.

Odo was of Frankish birth: his father was a man

[1] Mabillon, *Ann. Ord. S. Bened.* iii. 330.

of exceptional education, whose knowledge of Justinian's laws made him much in demand as an adjudicator of public quarrels. Odo became a page in the court of Duke William of Aquitaine, the future founder of Cluny. Between the years of sixteen and nineteen he suffered from painful ill-health, which only found relief when he devoted himself to St Martin of Tours. Near the church of that saint he lived apart in a cell, and gave himself to study. Then he spent some time at Paris for his further education. Returning to Tours he found a copy of St Benedict's Rule, and this he followed for three years though not yet a monk. He was thirty years old when he came to Berno at Beaume: he was just in time to be one of the group of monks who started the new house of Cluny. Towards the end of his life Berno got Odo elected as his successor; but in his will he found it necessary to divide the houses of his foundation, leaving Beaume with its still dissentient monks to his kinsman Wido, and Cluny, incomplete as yet and very poor, to Odo.

The inception of the Burgundian reform was thus due to the zeal of Berno. Cluny from the first was dominated by the Customs of Benedict of Aniane, and it was placed under the direct protection of the papal see. Its fame for holiness was already widespread before Berno's death, but its influence as a centre of monastic revival begins with the rule of Odo (927–41). Under a special papal sanction Odo undertook the reform of other houses, some of which became priories of Cluny, though the majority remained

independent.   His amazing activities extended
over the whole of France and a great part of Italy
as well.

The abbey of Fleury on the Loire, which claimed
to have the body of the great St Benedict, had
been devastated by the Northmen.   Its possessions were thereafter usurped by the neighbouring
nobles.   For some years it had been without an
abbot, and the monks were entirely undisciplined,
eating meat and riding out with arms: such goods
as the monastery still retained they divided
among themselves, instead of holding them as
a common fund.   About 930 Count Elisiardus
received the abbey from the French king Raoul
(Rudolf), and he called on Odo to reform it.   On
his arrival with certain counts and bishops, the
monks fortified their house and refused admittance for three days.   At length Odo at peril of
his life entered alone, and by his courage and
gentleness won them over.   It was however only
with difficulty that he persuaded them to abandon
their private property and accept the discipline
on which he insisted.   But Fleury was worth
winning.   When Pope Leo VII confirmed its
reform in 938, he said: 'It is our hope that if
religious observance shall again flourish in that
monastery, the very head of all, then the houses
round about, which are as members of the body,
will recover their strength.'   This prognostication
was amply fulfilled, and Fleury soon began to vie
with Cluny as a new centre of reform.

Another movement of monastic revival was in
full progress in Lower Lorraine, during the very

years in which Odo was active in France and Italy.
Gerard of Brogne, near Namur, came of a Frankish
family with high connexions. Like Odo, and like
our own St Dunstan, he was brought up in a court.
He was a page of Count Béranger of Namur, who
presently took him into his secret counsels and
entrusted him with affairs of delicacy and importance. But his soul was vexed by the grievous
state of the Church, and he devoted his property
at Brogne to the erection of a college of canons.
Then a visit to Paris, on a mission from the count
of Namur to the great Count Robert, brought him
to the monastery of St Denys of which Robert
himself was lay abbot. He obtained the body of
St Eugenius, then resting at Paris, for his new
church at Brogne which had been begun in the
previous year, 914. Returning to St Denys he
studied the monastic life and repaired the neglect
of his education. He now determined to sub-
stitute monks for the clerks whom he had introduced at Brogne. His new foundation he made
over to the abbey of St Denys, from which he
brought twelve monks. He himself took the
monastic vow and became their abbot: he was
ordained priest by the bishop of Paris in 927.
Desiring further seclusion he appointed priors to
manage the house, and retired to a cell near the
church. But his fame spread, and soon he was
called upon by Giselbert, duke of Lorraine, to
reform St Ghislain, where there were clerks of an
ill conversation, who had carried their saint about,
singing and begging, till he got himself stolen.
Gerard recovered the saint at Maubeuge; the duke

started a monastery, and restored the alienated estates.

A wider responsibility now awaited him. Arnulf, count of Flanders, was one of the strong personalities of his time. His father Baldwin, a Carolingian by descent, had married K. Alfred's daughter Ælfthryth. Monasticism was practically extinct in his dominion. The two most notable abbeys had been those of St Peter (*Blandinium*) and St Bavo, neighbouring houses at Ghent. St Bavo was a desolate ruin: at St Peter's there were a few clerks, and Count Arnulf was lay abbot. The abbey next in importance was St Bertin's at St Omer: here there were monks indeed, but with no regular life, under Arnulf's brother Adalolf as their lay abbot, and after his death under Arnulf himself. Bishop Trancmar of Noyon, whose diocese then included that of Térouanne, urged Count Arnulf to rebuild the abbey of St Bavo. Gerard of Brogne was called upon in the year 937 to undertake the reform of both the abbeys at Ghent. The count authorized him to do the like for all the other monasteries of Flanders, and in 944 St Bertin was taken in hand. Here the monks who were still in possession stoutly resisted, and at length departed in a body. The populace was much moved, and the count followed the monks, entreating them to return and submit. In the end nine of them yielded, but the majority took ship for England, where they were hospitably received by the king and were given the abbey of Bath. Folcwin, the chronicler of St Bertin, who records this migration, says that K. Athelstan thus welcomed them on the ground that his brother

Edwin, who was drowned at sea in 933, had been buried in their abbey by the order of Adalolf the lay abbot of that time: but in fact K. Athelstan was dead, and his brother Edmund was on the throne. Gerard filled the abbey of St Bertin with monks drawn from all quarters; and then, as he was needed at Ghent, he left it under the temporary control of Agilo a monk from St Évre at Toul, and of Womar a monk of Blandinium who afterwards became abbot at Ghent and received St Dunstan there.[1]

In the meantime a movement in Upper Lorraine had been initiated under wholly different conditions. This district, lying between the rival kingdoms to the west and to the east, had been continually changing sides; and to the troubles

---

[1] When Gerard of Brogne retired from his control of the monasteries of Flanders in 953, he appointed Womar in his place with general powers of supervision. Womar became actual abbot of Blandinium and St Bavo at Ghent, but only with difficulty maintained his position in the latter; for between the two houses there was a somewhat fierce rivalry. His death is variously placed between 980 and 982. In the A.-S. Chron. C (Abingdon) it is given under 981 ('Womær, abbud on Gent'). In the *Liber Vitae* of New Minster, in a list of brethren of the Old Minster who are to be prayed for in the New, we read: 'Domnus abba Uuomarus, qui olim cenobio Gent prelatus hanc devotus adiit gentem, huiusque se familie precibus humillime commendavit' (Birch, p. 24).

It would seem, therefore, that Abbot Womar, by whom Dunstan had been received in his exile, afterwards paid a visit to England, and asked for the prayers of the Old Minster at Winchester. He may even have helped in the compilation of the *Regularis Concordia*. His mention in the Abingdon Chronicle might suggest that he died in England—possibly at Abingdon. But he appears to have been buried at Blandinium (Mabillon, *Ann. Bened.* iv. 8).

thus caused had been added the horrors of a Hungarian invasion. The monasteries had been deserted and ruined: their lands had fallen to the bishops, and not as elsewhere to the king or the nobles; and the bishops had been compelled to distribute them among the armed retainers on whom they relied for protection. Reform was thus faced with peculiar difficulties, as the bishops were unwilling to promote it. It came in time from no one leader, but from a group of clergy and others, who were shocked by the scandalous condition of the Church, and one after another sought to amend their own lives by self-imposed severities or by retirement into a hermit's life. Presently a considerable body of them united to urge on the bishops the restoration of the monasteries. In 933 Adalbero the bishop of Metz, threatened by the proposed departure of a number of the new enthusiasts to found a monastic home for themselves in Southern Italy, was moved to action. He consented to the reconstruction of the abbey of Gorze, promising to restore its lands so far as he could recover the possession of them. Einold the archdeacon of Toul was the first abbot, and a beginning was made in circumstances of extreme hardship. He was ably supported by the notable John of Gorze, one of the keenest of the reforming spirits, who succeeded him as abbot after his death in 959.[1] The next abbey to be revived was St Èvre (S. *Aper*) of Toul. Gauzlin

---

[1] The detailed narrative of this movement forms a fascinating section of the Life of John of Gorze, written by his friend John abbot of St Arnulf at Metz, cc. 9–39 (*Monum. Germ. SS.* iv. 335; Migne, *P. L.* 137, 242 ff.).

the bishop of Toul paid a visit to Fleury and brought back St Benedict's Rule and a code of Customs. The first abbot (934) was Archembold, who indeed may have come from Fleury; for it would seem that he was afterwards abbot there from 942 to 945. We have already noted that Gerard of Brogne left St Bertin's abbey in charge of Agilo a monk of Toul as well as of Womar; and putting this and other facts together we may fairly conclude that, different as the three movements were in their origin, the monastic observance in all of them had a common basis in the Customs of Benedict of Aniane.[1] It would seem that Gorze, where excessive austerities after the Eastern model were at first in vogue, soon modified its practice by the more reasonable example of Toul.

We learn from this rapid review that on the Continent in the early part of the tenth century three movements, distinct in origin and independent at the outset, were bringing about the revival of the monastic life, which had been almost crushed out of existence by the dreadful calamities of the times. Its old homes were for the most part in ruins; the lands were held by intruders ; a few monks remained here and there, but under lay abbots their discipline and learning had almost wholly disappeared: many of the surviving churches were served only by clerks. When strong and earnest spirits once again heard the call to a life of complete dedication, the past

---

[1] It is not without significance that the best MS of Benedict of Aniane's *Concordia Regularum* (Orleans, 233) is of the first half of the tenth century, and was preserved (if not written) at Fleury (Plenkers, in Traube's *Quellen u. Unters.* i. 3, 13).

came to their aid. St Benedict's plain and spiritual Rule presented the ideal and marked out the general lines of the common life; and the labour of his great namesake, Benedict of Aniane, who under Charlemagne and his successor had elaborated a complete code of Customs for the application of the Rule to the details of every day and every hour, began to bear fruit anew after a century of neglect and oblivion, and afforded the common basis on which the various reforming codes were to be built up.[1]

What had happened abroad was now to happen in England. Alfred had realized the need of such a revival, and had done what he could by introducing monks of piety and learning from across the sea: but his effort had signally failed. A native movement alone could succeed, and of this there was no sign. But when a man of high position and inspiring personality felt the need, not for others only but for himself, and could not rest until he had sacrificed his all for the humble life of poverty and obedience and entire devotion to God; then here in England as elsewhere his zeal was contagious, kindred spirits came about him, and before long postulants were pressing for admittance to the restored homes of the religious life.

[1] In the foregoing sketch I have relied mainly on Sackur's valuable work, *Die Cluniacenser*, vol. i, 1902. A clear account of St Benedict of Aniane, and his attempt in 817 to secure absolute uniformity of observance in all monastic houses, will be found in Edmund Bishop's essay on 'The Origin of the Prymer' (*Liturgica Historica*, pp. 222 ff.; reprinted from *Early English Text Society's Publications*, Orig. Ser. no. 109, 1897). See also below, p. 149.

VII

THE *REGULARIS CONCORDIA*

It is impossible to do justice to the English monastic revival of the tenth century, if we content ourselves with its external history and with the ecclesiastical careers of its great leaders. It is indeed in regard to the external history that misapprehension has been so great as to demand a fresh investigation of the sources from which alone it can be safely drawn. But, when criticism and reconstruction have to some extent done their work, we find ourselves still wholly uninstructed as to the inner life of the monasteries, and unable to appreciate the stage in the long development of Benedictine monachism which this particular reform represents. Of all this we might have remained helplessly ignorant, if time had not spared to us the great literary monument of the movement, the code of Customs which bears the title: *Regularis Concordia Anglicae nationis monachorum sanctimonialiumque.*

This work was printed by Clement Reyner in the appendix to his *Apostolatus Benedictinorum in Anglia* (Douai, 1626). It is reprinted thence in the first volume of the *Monasticon Anglicanum* (1817), and will be found also in Migne, *P. L.* cxxxvii. The best edition is that of W. S. Logeman in *Anglia* (Neue Folge, I), where it is printed from B. M. *Tib.* A 3 for the sake of its interlinear Old

English translation ; but Logeman has not used the other equally important MS, *Faustina* B 3. It is certainly not creditable to our English scholarship that there is no handy edition, no critical text. We may hope, however, that our need will ere long be supplied by a Benedictine monk of Downside. Mention must here be made of a summary of the great work, which Abbot Ælfric wrote for the monks of Eynsham, and which was printed by Miss Bateson in Dean Kitchin's *Obedientiary Rolls of St Swithun's Winchester* (Hampshire Record Society, 1892).

What then is the *Regularis Concordia*? Its preface will give us in general terms the answer.

The glorious K. Edgar, we are told, was guided in his youth by the counsels of a certain abbot, who explained to him the royal road [1] of the catholic faith. So when he came to the throne he was grieved at the ruin of the monasteries throughout his realm: he set himself to restore them and to cast out the foul abominations of neglectful clerks, establishing abbeys both for men and for women: of the former he himself was protector as 'pastorum pastor', while the latter he committed to the guardianship of Ælfryth his wife. In all alike the Rule of St Benedict was duly honoured: abbots and abbesses with the brothers and sisters under them sought in eager rivalry to follow in the footsteps of the saints, with one faith indeed, but not with one customary use ('una fide, non tamen uno consuetudinis usu'). The king therefore assembled a synodal council ('synodale concilium') at

---

[1] The expression 'regia via' is used again below in such a way as to suggest that it has special reference to the monastic life: 'qui viam regiam mandatorum domini absque jactantiae vitio lactei adhuc humiliter incedunt.'

Winchester. To this he sent a letter of exhortation in humble terms, urging all to come to an agreement in one common use, following the holy and approved fathers and strictly observing the precepts of the Rule;[1] lest the unequal and divergent use of one and the same Rule in one and the same country should prove occasion of scandal.

The national note, which is the unique characteristic of this code of Customs, is thus struck at the outset—King and Country, *rex et patria*.

The assembly fervently welcomed the message of the king, and bearing in mind the advice given by our holy patron Gregory to the blessed Augustine, that he should establish in the young Church of the English good customs not only of the Roman Church, but also of the Churches of Gaul, they called in monks of the monastery of St Benedict at Fleury, and also of that famous monastery known by the name of Ghent. Thus they sought and found a way of great devotion, tempered with much subtle discretion of reason.[2] Their conclusions they set out in this small volume.

Here we recognize the national aptitude for taking the best from all quarters, tempering extravagance with a fine discretion, adapting rather than copying the customs of other lands.

Then, lest individuals by acting on their own pre-

[1] 'Ut concordes aequali consuetudinis usu, sanctos probatosque imitando patres, regularia praecepta tenaci mentis ancora servantes'. The words *concordes* and *regularia praecepta* give the clue to the title *Regularis concordia Anglicae nationis*, especially when taken with what follows: 'ne impar ac varius unius regulae ac unius patriae usus probrose vituperium sacrae conversationi irrogaret'.

[2] 'Amabili . . . impleri devotione, temperata cum magna atque subtili rationis discretione'.

sumptuous choice should forfeit the fruits of obedience, they bound themselves by a solemn vow to observe these Customs in their common practice, whilst all should be free to use in secret parts of the church such private prayers as the Holy Spirit might inspire.   Moreover Dunstan, the noble archbishop of this country ('egregius hujus patriae archiepiscopus'), in confirming the work of the synod, added a caution as to the dealings of monks with convents of women.   And this one thing we have thought should be looked to, namely that the customary prayers for the king and our benefactors should not be said too fast, lest they move God to anger rather than to mercy.   If necessity should call for some addition to the common use, this may be permitted for a time: otherwise nothing further is to be done without synodical sanction.

Thus far the preface in its earliest form.   There follow a number of additional paragraphs dealing with various points of detail.   Though probably contemporary, they are marked off from what has preceded in two ways: first, as appearing in a different order in our two MSS; and secondly by certain small points of style which seem to indicate a different writer; the same characteristics of style recur in the brief epilogue with which in one only of the MSS the book closes.

We cannot date this synodal council of Winchester: we know nothing of it beyond what we have learned from this preface.   The king evidently was not present: possibly Dunstan was not, if we may judge from the terms in which he is referred to.   The hand that drew up the document was doubtless that of Ethelwold.   Ælfric in sending his summary of the code to the monks of Eynsham says explicitly that Ethelwold with his fellow bishops and abbots collected these Customs from various quarters and established their observance.[1] But it is generally held that, if the hand be Ethelwold's, the inspiring mind is that of Dunstan himself.

The intention of such a code of Customs as the *Regularis Concordia* presents to us was to supplement the simple Rule of St Benedict and to adapt its provisions to the wholly different circumstances in which after the lapse of some four centuries monastic life was to be carried on. St Benedict had put forth regulations for a community of lay monks, drawn mainly from the class of agricultural labourers in Italy. He had given them a time-table in which divine service in church— the *opus Dei*—was indeed the first consideration: but though the services were many, beginning at 2 a.m. and distributed over the day until Compline was said at sun-set, the whole time occupied by them was not much more than four hours. Three to four hours were devoted to reading and meditation, and the rest of the day was filled with field-labour and other manual work. Two or three of the brethren were in priest's orders, and there was mass on Sundays and festivals, but not on other days. In the last quarter of the

---

[1] Obedientiary Rolls, *ut supr.* : 'Ideoque hęc pauca de libro consuetudinum, quam sanctus aðelwoldus uuintoniensis episcopus cum coepiscopis et abbatibus tempore eadgari felicissimi regis anglorum undique collegit ac monachis instituit observandum, scriptitando demonstro, eo quod hactenus predictus libellus uestrę fraternitati incognitus habetur'.

eighth century, as we learn from Paul Warnefrid's Commentary on the Rule, field labour had largely been abandoned; there were servants in the garden and kitchen, though some manual work was still done by all; and there was a daily conventual mass. New ideals had entered into the lives of monks, and monasteries were the homes of learning and education. Many, if not most, of the monks were ordained or on the way to ordination as priests.

The eighth century was a bright period of devotion and learning in the English Church—as witness Bede and the school of York which produced Alcuin. Abroad there was desolation and darkness, until Charlemagne arose to bring in a new era. With that great reformer's activities we are not here concerned, save only with his effort to revive monasticism. It is perhaps worth noting that it was no code of Customs that he sought to impose: it was the neglect of the Rule itself that he was fain to deal with. In the Annals of Lauresham we are told that at a certain synod he assembled all the abbots and monks who were in attendance; they met together and read the Rule of the holy father Benedict, and they pledged themselves that, whatever in monasteries or in monks was found contrary to the Rule, this they would amend in accordance with that Rule.[1]

---

[1] 'Similiter in ipso synodo congregavit universos abbates et monachos qui ibi aderant, et ipsi inter se conventum faciebant, et legerunt regulam sancti patris Benedicti, et eam tradiderunt sapientes in conspectu abbatum et monachorum: et tunc jussu ejus generaliter super omnes episcopos,

But, as Alfred found a hundred years later, monasticism cannot be made to flourish by the *ipse dixit* of a prince. Only a great personality, himself devoted to this way of serving God, could make a fresh beginning and remodel the ancient institute to meet the needs of a new age. Then came St Benedict of Aniane, the second founder, as he has been called, of the Benedictine Order.

Beginning, as many a reformer did, with exceptional austerities, he would speak, as his biographer Ardo tells us, of St Benedict's Rule as meant for the tyro and the weak; and he looked to the East as offering the highest ideal in the precepts of St Basil and the rule of St Pachomius. He drew up a collection of ancient rules which still remains; but in practice it was St Benedict's Rule with modifications and accretions which was the basis of his reform. Liturgical additions helped to occupy the time of monks who were no longer engaged to any great extent in manual work. Of these accessory practices the most certainly his own, and the most abiding in after times, was the recital of the fifteen gradual psalms, in three divisions with prayers after each, before the usual service of Nocturns. Other new practices are with less certainty attributed to him. But what chiefly characterized his endeavour after

abbates, presbyteros, diacones seu universo clero facta est, ut unusquisque in loco suo juxta constitutionem sanctorum patrum ... et quicquid in monasteriis seu in monachis contra regulam sancti Benedicti factum fuisset hoc ipsud juxta ipsam regulam sancti Benedicti emendare fecissent,' *Annal. Lauresham.* xxv (Pertz, i. 38).

reform was the determination to enforce absolute uniformity upon all monks everywhere—uniformity in food, in dress, in occupation, in worship. His great day came when Charlemagne had passed away and Louis the Pious came to the throne. The Council of 817 was his triumph, but it was a short-lived success. Not only was such centralization as he aimed at impossible in the break-up of the Empire; but in itself it was a contradiction of the ruling principle of the great St Benedict, that each monastery should be a family with the abbot as its father and independent ruler, a family among families whose only link was the observance of the Rule. St Benedict of Aniane failed in the task on which his heart was set; but his work was not lost, his ideas were destined to mould in various ways the movements of reform which sprang up in the tenth century. Cluny was to carry them to the farthest extreme, with exaggerated liturgical amplifications, and with a system of centralization which under an exceptional succession of able and long-lived abbots gave it for two centuries a dominating influence in the Church and in the world.

There is an ancient tract, now generally known from the opening words of its title as the *Ordo Qualiter*—the Order how brethren in a monastery should live and serve God. It certainly belongs to the period before the reform of Benedict of Aniane. It knows nothing of his special devotion of the fifteen psalms with threefold prayer. It makes no mention of a daily mass, and indeed it adds little if anything to the simple services prescribed by the Rule. The *Regularis Concordia* begins by embodying a great part of the opening section of this *Ordo Qualiter*—that, namely, which describes the common routine (the services and times for reading, work and food) of an ordinary week-day. After a preliminary admonition that all undertakings must be begun with a benediction, the compiler at once gives us the very words of the *Ordo Qualiter*.

Dom Bruno Albers, who has published five volumes of *Consuetudines Monasticae*, prints the *Ordo Qualiter* in vol. III. His text, which he has taken from a single MS, varies greatly from that of the MSS which he cites in the apparatus. If we follow the readings of the MSS which he calls *a* and *a*[1], we shall find a much closer agreement with the text of the *Regularis Concordia*; and we may note that *a*[1] in particular has points which link it with MSS preserved in England.[1] It may be said in passing that a great debt is owed to Dom Albers for his immense collection of materials; but his judgements, especially those which are expressed in a dissertation published before half of his work was completed,[2] must be received with considerable caution.

Now, whereas the *Regularis Concordia* follows

---

[1] I have noted this for various points in *Tiberius* A 3, *Harl.* 5431, C.C.C. Camb. 57, and Camb. Univ. Libr. Ll. i. 14. The codex *a*[1] is Barbarini xiv. 19.

[2] *Untersuchungen z. den ältesten Mönchsgewohnheiten* (Munich, 1905). Valuable criticism of a constructive character will be found in Dom U. Berlière's articles in the *Revue Bénédictine* for 1906, 1908, and 1912.

the *Ordo Qualiter* in the opening section, it makes large insertions from point to point, which illustrate that elaboration of accessory devotions which was characteristic of the new reform and was in part the heritage of the Carolingian reform under Benedict of Aniane. Thus before the service of Nocturns, which began about 2 a.m., the monk on arriving in church is to kneel in a fitting place and pray silently with great compunction and recollection of sins: then he is to say the seven penitential psalms—the first three to be followed by the Lord's Prayer as a prayer for himself, and by the thanksgiving for protection during the night which is prescribed in the *Ordo Qualiter*: the next two, followed by the prayer for the king and benefactors: the last two, followed by prayer for the faithful departed. Presently, when all are seated in their places, he will say the fifteen psalms, divided into three groups by intervals of prayer as before—the devotion which was specially connected with St Benedict of Aniane. Then comes the service of Nocturns. Then two psalms are added, one for the king, the other for the king and queen and benefactors, with appropriate collects: and this addition, we are told, is to be made at the end of all the regular hours. After an interval in summer time will come Lauds of the day. Then after the *Miserere* and two psalms with prayers for the king, and for king, queen and benefactors, they are to sing antiphons of Holy Cross, the Blessed Virgin, and the saint or dedication of the church. Then they go singing in procession to a chapel for Lauds of

All Saints, followed by Lauds of the dead. Then at day-break follows Prime, after which come psalms and collects, a litany, the Lord's prayer, a psalm and prayers. After all this is a space for reading, 'according to the precept of the Rule'. To pass on to the evening, there is again an elaboration of devotions: before Vespers there are private prayers; after Vespers of the day come Vespers of All Saints, Vespers of the dead, Matins of the dead. When we have added to all this Terce and the Matin Mass, reading and prayers in the chapter-house, Sext, the principal Mass, None and Compline, we shall see that not much energy, or even time, was left for other occupations than those of devotion.

A comparison with continental codes of Customs will show that the English monks were not more heavily burdened than their foreign brethren of the tenth century, except perhaps in the many prayers for the royal house, in respect of which the *Regularis Concordia* holds a position quite unique. Cluny, if not already, yet soon afterwards, went further still on the path of elaboration, developing to excess the music and the ceremonial of the services.

The first chapter, which is thus built up on the foundation of the *Ordo Qualiter*, is concerned with the *feria*, or ordinary week-day, with brief notes as to changes made on Sundays and festivals. The second chapter begins a long series of instructions as to the ritual special to various festivals throughout the year. The *Ordo Qualiter* is no longer a guide. As to other sources we can here only note that the interesting usages observed in connexion with the *Tenebrae* on Good Friday and the dramatic rite on the night of the Resurrection find a close parallel in the Verdun customs; and that certain points of detail suggest a relation with the customs of Einsiedeln, where indeed before the close of the tenth century an Englishman named Gregory was the abbot. But the investigation of sources is a task which has hardly yet begun; and it is much hampered by the fact that we have no secure testimony to the use of Fleury at the time when the *Regularis Concordia* was drawn up.[1]

We have little to help us in forming a conception of the monastic life as revived by St Dunstan at Glastonbury during the fruitful period of from ten to fifteen years in which he was abbot there, before his exile had brought him into contact with the continental reform at Ghent. But we shall perhaps be not far from the truth if we think of it as not more complicated than the life prescribed in the *Ordo Qualiter* of the seventh or eighth century, with which he may very possibly have been acquainted.[2]

Now the preface to the *Regularis Concordia*, when carefully studied, is found to contain certain expressions indicative of a critical situation.

[1] See Dom Thomas Symons in the *Downside Review* for January 1922 (XL 15 ff.), where a useful beginning is made.

[2] The very prominence accorded to the injunctions of the *Ordo Qualiter* which we have remarked in the opening section of the *Regularis Concordia* may even suggest that this manual was already familiar and had acquired a certain sanction from long use.

The new foundations, stimulated by contact with eager representatives of foreign types of observance (Fleury, Corbey, Ghent), had begun to vie with one another in excellency of devotional practice— *sanctorum sequi vestigia, una fide, non tamen uno consuetudinis usu, certatim cum magna studuerunt hilaritate.* It was a zeal without wisdom, which threatened to produce discord. It called for a strong remedy. And here perhaps we may trace the moderating strength of the great archbishop, who knew by his own long experience that these modern elaborations were by no means essential to a true monastic life; who indeed had come to know them only after his special work at Glastonbury was ended. If it be true, as in deference to general consent we have been ready to allow, that St Dunstan's was the mind that inspired the *Regularis Concordia,* though St Ethelwold's was the hand that drew it up, it is most true in the sense that it was the statesman archbishop who foresaw the danger of an embittered rivalry, and sought to impose a reasonable limit—*ut concordes aequali consuetudinis usu . . . nullo modo dissentiendo discordarent ; ne impar ac varius unius regulae ac unius patriae usus probrose vituperium sanctae conversationi irrogaret.* The words of warning are said to come from the letter of the king; but the king's speech is the speech of his chief minister.

In this light we can understand more easily the words which record the obligation undertaken by all the abbots and abbesses alike—that, while life should last, being subject to the yoke of the Rule, they would observe those customs that follow openly in their common practice. But none the less in secret parts of the church special devotions might be used within reasonable limits by any who were moved to adopt them.[1] A later paragraph makes provision for additions to the public devotions suggested by a temporary need; but these are to be used only while the need lasts: apart from this new usages may not be established without formal sanction.[2]

If this be a true account of the situation, we need not vex ourselves with the question whether the fully elaborated scheme of daily services and devotions was expected to be of absolute obligation in all monasteries, or whether it was not from the first regarded as the ideal for houses which aimed at the highest observance. It is certainly instructive to find that Ælfric, the devoted pupil of St Ethelwold, felt himself free to draw up for the monks of Eynsham, who had not a copy of the *Regularis Concordia* itself, a scheme of devotions based indeed on the great code, but somewhat less exacting in detail: it contains no mention, for example, of the daily recitation of the fifteen gradual psalms.

[1] 'Unanimes voverunt . . . se vita comite jugo regulae deditos has adnotatas morum consuetudines communi palam custodire conversatione: caeterum unusquisque secretis oratorii locis, in quantum spiritus sancti gratia clementer instigaverit, peculiaribus, teste deo, cum bonorum operum vigilantia, consulte utatur orationibus.'

[2] 'Nequaquam ulterius praesumptuose usu teneatur temerario, nisi concilio synodali electum traditumque cum discretione virtutum omnium matre ab universis fuerit catholicis.'

It remains true, at any rate, that such was the ideal which the reform movement of the tenth century ultimately proposed for the monasteries of England. It differed only in points of detail from the scheme of life and worship which was at the same time generally approved by all the reformed monasteries of the Continent. We have noted its divergence from the system established by the great St Benedict for his simple Italian monks. In spite of occasional protests it ruled monasticism for two centuries. At length in the twelfth century the extravagant ritual and ceremonial of Cluny produced the Cistercian reaction. Modern Benedictinism has learned its lesson and has cut away most of the devotional accretions of the mediæval period, and has arrived at a reasonable mean which is not incompatible with literary labours and educational activities.

It is interesting to note the judgement recently passed by Abbot Butler on the development of which we have been speaking:

In chapter XVII about four hours daily was estimated as a probable average time for the total common service of God in choir according to St Benedict's horarium, and certainly it was not much more. But in mediæval monasteries it must have taken up many more hours than this: indeed much the greater portion of the working hours must have been passed in church, as is now done by the monks of the Greek Church. It can hardly be supposed that nothing but piety prompted the change. The cause probably was this: manual labour had been given up; relatively few men, even Benedictine monks, are students such as will spend several hours a day in reading, and in the early Middle Ages the difficulties as .

to books and libraries must have been nearly prohibitive; consequently, as some way had to be found of filling up the time, the monks were kept in the church nearly all day to give them something to do and keep them occupied.[1]

Let this be said in conclusion. If the English reformers were led by their foreign advisers into an exaggeration of devotional practices which experience was destined to condemn, it is to be remembered in their favour that their zeal did not take the far more objectionable form of excessive bodily austerities. In this they were, as the *Regularis Concordia* sufficiently attests, true to the spirit of the founder of their order. Individuals like St Ethelwold might be severe with themselves in the matter of abstinence, but they did not attempt to make their own practice the rule for others. Diet was simple, but sufficient; the time allowed for sleep was ample; the life was disciplined, but not austere. And in spite of the long hours in church, manuscripts were written and splendidly illuminated, the sciences of the day were cultivated, and the voluminous writings of Ælfric mark an era in our Old English literature.

[1] *Benedictine Monachism*, p. 296.

ADDITIONAL NOTE A

ON THE 'POSTSCRIPT' TO THE ENGLISH VERSION OF THE RULE

COCKAYNE at the end of his *Leechdoms* (Rolls Ser., iii. 433 ff.) has printed a curious document which stands as a postscript to the Anglo-Saxon translation of St Benedict's Rule in the Cotton MS, *Faustina* A 10. The MS is assigned by Dr Schröer to the end of the eleventh or the beginning of the twelfth century. This 'postscript' is preserved only in a fragmentary condition. The beginning is lost, and also a considerable portion of the text further on: the piece, as we have it, starts after a blank space in the middle of a page; whence we conclude that the scribe was copying from a manuscript already mutilated.

This *Faustina* MS differs from all other extant copies of the A.-S. version: for whereas they present the Latin and English texts alternately chapter by chapter, here on the contrary we find no Latin text at all. Moreover, in the preface and in one chapter we have matter foreign to the Rule and derived from other sources.

Cockayne was of opinion that the writer of the 'postscript' was St Ethelwold himself, the translator of the Rule; and this view appears to be generally accepted. Dr Schröer is convinced that the writer was an abbot, and therefore, if he were St Ethelwold, he must have written before 963, the year in which St Ethelwold became bishop of Winchester. The question of authorship is not unimportant, as this fragmentary piece contains historical statements the value of which must depend on the date to which they are assigned. For example, Cockayne himself pointed to one such statement in the following words: 'The Liber de Hyda and William of

Malmsbury attribute to king Edred the enlargement of the monastic foundation at Abingdon, which we here learn on the authority of Æþelwold himself, who was a party in the transactions, to be due to Eadgar' (p. 417). This one discrepancy should give us pause: for it is not only the authorities named by Cockayne that must be thrown over, if K. Edgar is to be accepted as the refounder of Abingdon, but also Ælfric's Life of St Ethelwold, 'Wulfstan's' revision of that Life, and the whole Abingdon tradition as represented in the *Chronicon Monasterii de Abingdon* with the allied documents published by Joseph Stevenson in two volumes of the Rolls Series. We must indeed rewrite a considerable portion of St Ethelwold's story, if we are to accept as his the following words of the 'postscript':[1] 'Before that there was but a scant number of monks in a few places in so great a kingdom, living by right rule. That was not more than in one place, called Glastonbury, where his father, king Eadmund, first established monks. From that place the aforesaid abbot was taken and ordained to the above mentioned monastery, which king Eadgar founded and furnished with monks.' It is difficult to imagine that St Ethelwold himself could have written thus, faithless to the memory of his patron K. Edred.[2]

Let us look, then, somewhat closely into this document, approaching it without any prepossession as to the question of its authorship, or even of its date. It would seem that not much has been lost at the beginning. It starts abruptly thus: '. . . world was mercifully filled with the light of the holy faith'. Then we are told of St Gregory's mission of St Augustine to England, and of the common life, like that of the first Christians, which was established by his orders and long survived in the minsters of the English race. All this comes ultimately

---

[1] I quote from Cockayne's translation, p. 439.

[2] We cannot suppose that 'Eadgar' is a scribal error for 'Eadred', since the whole context forbids it.

from Bede.   Then with the word 'But' the narrative is broken off, and a considerable portion is missing: for when it is resumed we find ourselves with Edgar and Dunstan.   We shall presently have to offer a conjecture as to one story which must have found a place in this gap.

The text proceeds: '(*Eadgar observing Dunstan*) understood and knew him a true director of his holy churches, before his *high character* was openly displayed to men. Hence he granted him multiplied and sufficient property and power.   Nor did he long delay, nor deprive him of authority.   It was not long before his brother (*Eadwig*) ended his days.   He, through his childish ignorance, parted this kingdom and divided its unity, and also distributed land of holy churches to strangers and robbers.'

Here we must pause for a moment, for we have come upon a statement for which there is not, so far as I know, any clear pre-Conquest evidence.   That K. Edwy was a robber of churches is indeed familiar enough to us from the pages of William of Malmesbury, but the legend is of gradual growth.   The anonymous biographer of St Oswald knows nothing of it, though he mentions the courage of Archbishop Oda in rebuking the king.   Ælfric's Life of St Ethelwold (*c.* 1005) does not mention Edwy. The Abingdon History has no word against him, even in its latest forms; but says that Ethelwold found great favour with him, and fills many pages with charters bearing this king's name (I. 169–254).   The first biographer of St Dunstan ('B.') does not charge Edwy with robbing churches, but throws the blame of his persecution of Dunstan and his friends upon 'that Jezabel' Ethelgifu (pp. 32 ff.):   still less is Edwy aspersed by the second biographer, Adelard (p. 59).

It is with Osbern of Canterbury, at the end of the eleventh century, that the charge begins to make its appearance.   The first biographer of St Dunstan had said that Ethelgifu had with the consent of the king brought under her control 'all the honour of that order and all the substance of its [or 'his ', that is Dunstan's] goods'.[1] The writer here, as too often, fails to use plain language; but the context does not suggest that any monastery but Glastonbury was touched. Osbern rewrites this boldly: 'And first, under stress of the king's edict, all the churches of monastic religion were spoiled of their property'.[2] Eadmer is much more careful, and says that all Dunstan's property in the monastery was ravaged and wasted, and he himself was driven into exile.[3] But William of Malmesbury follows Osbern and exaggerates his statement: through the whole of England went these terrible edicts, monks were proscribed and their monasteries confiscated (p. 284). Elsewhere he repeats the statement, and declares that his own monastery at Malmesbury was made 'stabulum clericorum'.[4]

Returning now to the statement of our writer, that K. Edwy 'distributed land of holy churches to strangers and robbers' (or, as perhaps it should be rendered, 'to ignorant plunderers'),[5] we might indeed pass it as a vague phrase with nothing more behind it than the recollection of the persecution of Dunstan: but it should set us on our guard, as being not what we should expect from an early writer, or from a writer whose interest was in Abingdon, to which K. Edwy would certainly seem to have been a benefactor.

If we read on, we find a long eulogy of K. Edgar, the terms of which recall the poem which introduces that

---

[1] 'Tunc illa ex predicti regis consensu omnem illius ordinis honorem omnemque subpellectilis sui substantiam suis legibus subjugavit' (p. 33).

[2] 'Et primo quidem urgente regis edicto omnes monasticae religionis ecclesiae suis rebus spoliabantur' (p. 101).

[3] 'Effecit namque apud regem ut cuncta quae in monasterio Dunstani habebantur diripi ac devastari . . . juberet' (p. 191).

[4] *Gesta Regum*, i. 163.

[5] 'Incuþum reaferum'.

king's reign in some of the manuscripts of the A.-S. Chronicle. Then comes a passage which clearly must refer to some story which had been told in the gap which precedes the mention of Edgar and Dunstan: 'As soon as he was chosen to his kingdom, he was very mindful of his promise, which he while a young child in his princely estate ('on his æþelincghade') made to God and to St Mary, when the abbot invited him to the monastic life ('þa se abbod hine gelaþode to þæm munuclife'). As we before said, by the recollection of his promise, in the beginning of his kingdom, he very thoughtfully began to improve the place ('þa stoþe'), as he before promised in his childhood . . . He soon gave order to have a glorious minster built there in three years' time. That will seem incredible to all who shall see that minster in after times and do not remember this. He commanded that same minster there ornamented to be consecrated to St Mary, to the praise and worship of God; and there he collected a great society of monks, that they should serve God according to the teaching of the holy rule.' Then comes the passage which we have already quoted, but which must be repeated here: 'Before that there was but a scant number of monks in a few places in so great a kingdom, living by right rule. That was not more than in one place, called Glastonbury, where his father, king Eadmund, first established monks. From that place the aforesaid abbot was taken and ordained to the above mentioned monastery, which king Eadgar founded and furnished with monks.'

Again we must ask, can we really suppose that a passage such as this could have been written by St Ethelwold, or indeed by any one conversant with the Abingdon tradition? We are not concerned to dispute the probability that St Ethelwold is the abbot and Abingdon the monastery to which reference is made: it is this very probability that makes us doubt the writer's knowledge either of Ethelwold or of Abingdon.

But what are we to say of the promise made by Edgar as an aetheling 'to God and to St Mary, when the abbot invited him to the monastic life'? We may recall the opening words of the preface to the *Regularis Concordia*, where K. Edgar is said to have shown tokens of piety from his earliest days under the guidance of a certain abbot who declared to him the royal road of the catholic faith—'abbate quodam assidue monente, ac regiam catholicae fidei viam demonstrante'. But it is clear that something much more definite is referred to in our passage. Some abbot, or some one who afterwards was an abbot and has been already mentioned, so that he can here be spoken of as 'the abbot', had shown him some definite place, some 'stowe' or ancient monastery, which the prince had then and there promised to restore, if ever it should be in his power.

The word 'munuclif', which Cockayne has translated quite legitimately 'the monastic life', has also the signification of 'monastery'.[1] It may be more reasonable to suppose that such is its meaning here: the abbot 'drew him to the monastery', rather than 'invited him to the monastic life'. But what we have said above is not dependent on the rendering of this particular sentence.

We may take it as certain that some story was contained in the lost portion of our document which would have made the allusion perfectly clear. What can it have been? There is nothing in the Abingdon tradition that helps us to an answer. But William of Malmesbury in his Life of St Dunstan (p. 290) tells us that Edgar in his earliest years contemplated a restoration of the monasteries. 'In fact', he says, 'as I have read in the prologue of a certain writer, who was setting out St Benet's Rule in English ('ut in cujusdam prologo legi

---

[1] Thus in Ælfric's Life of St Swithhun (*Lives*, i. 468): 'Eadgar cynincg . . . fela munuclifa arærde'; and A.-S. Chron E, *s.a.* 975: 'Ælfere ealdorman het towurpon swyðe manig munuclif þe Eadgar cyng . . .', and Plummer's note (ii. 163)

qui regulam Benedicti Anglico enucleabat fuso '), while on a certain day he was exercising himself with bow and arrows, he discovered some great buildings in the distance, which were in ruins, and asked his companions what this might be.' He learned that it was all that remained of a monastery destroyed by war or the tyranny of kings: 'then lifting his eyes toward heaven he bound himself with a promise that if ever he should come to the throne, he would restore this and other monasteries to their ancient condition'.

Here is just the story that we want, though no abbot is mentioned in it: that is a detail of little import, since William of Malmesbury is only telling the story from memory. But he says that he found it in the Prologue to an English version of the Rule. Was that Prologue, as a matter of fact, the very piece which has hitherto been called a 'postscript', because it stands without its opening sentences at the end of a copy of the translation of the Rule? We leave this as a suggestion only for the present, and go forward with the study of our document.

The writer goes on to speak of K. Edgar as following the admonitions of Archbishop Dunstan and proceeding in the matter of reform. 'He cleansed holy places (halige stoþa) from foulnesses of all men, not only in the kingdom of the West Saxons, but also in the land of the Mercians. For example, he drove out the canons (canonicas), who were more then sufficiently notorious for the aforesaid crimes; and in the most important places (stoþum) of all his dominion he established monks to perform a reverential service to the Saviour Christ. In some places also he established mynchens, and entrusted them to his consort Ælfþrið, that at every need she should help them. He ever investigated, himself, about the right conversation of monks, and kindly advised her to imitate him, and in the same way to see to the mynchens.'

Here we are again reminded of the preface to the

Regularis Concordia, where we read that K. Edgar, finding that many monasteries were in ruins and almost destitute of divine service, restored them everywhere and cast out the foulnesses of negligent clerks: he introduced not monks only but mynchens as well, setting over them fathers and mothers. He himself, in fulfilment of his royal duty, as 'pastorum pastor' protected the flocks which by God's grace he had gathered together; and to his wife Ælfthryth he entrusted the protection of the mynchens. All alike lived by St Benet's Rule.

Our author in like manner proceeds at once to speak of the Rule. K. Edgar, he continues, 'began with earnest scrutiny to seek out and inquire concerning the precepts of the holy Rule, and was willing to know the instruction of the Rule itself . . . From a desire of this wisdom he ordered the translation of this Rule from Latin into English. Although the acute and wise men . . . have no occasion for this English translation; it is however a necessity for unlearned secular men, who . . . turn unto their Lord, and choose the holy service of this Rule . . . I then have reckoned this translation to make much difference. Well may it be of no consequence with what language a man is begotten unto God and allured to the true faith, provided only that he do come unto God. Unlearned natives therefore may have the knowledge of the holy Rule, through an explanation in their own language . . . Hence then I with all devotion pray my successors and intreat in the Lord's name, that they ever increase the observance of this holy Rule . . .'

Let us note here first the statement that the Rule was translated by K. Edgar's orders. This is in harmony with the tradition preserved in the *Liber Eliensis*, that the translation was made by St Ethelwold, who received in recompense an estate from the king and his queen Ælfthryth. Next let us observe that our author does not claim to be the translator, but only defends the practical usefulness of the translation. Such words do not guide us to any particular abbot or any particular monastery. Indeed they may have been written either by an abbot or by a bishop, who was commending the translation to his abbey or to abbeys under his charge. The writer proceeds to warn his successors against diminishing 'the patrimony of God', and includes abbesses also in his admonition ('We also teach abbesses . . .'); and he ends with an imprecation against any one, potentate or king, who shall alienate the properties of churches.

It remains to call attention to a point of detail, which will be examined more fully at a later point.[1] In a passage cited above the writer says that K. Edgar 'drove out the canons (*canonicas*)'. But all our tenth-century documents use the term 'priests' or 'clerks' (preostas, *clericos*). It was this point of detail which first made me suspicious of the attribution of our fragment to St Ethelwold as its author. I think that I have now shown other and yet stronger reasons why the piece cannot have come from his pen.

To sum up: the fragmentary document, which is copied out at the end of the English version of the Rule in *Faustina* A 10, probably stood in an earlier MS as the prologue to this unique form of the version, which beside other peculiarities offers a continuous English text, not broken by alternating chapters of the Latin. This prologue contained in a section now lost a story of K. Edgar's promise made in his youth to restore, if he came to the throne, a certain monastery, the ruins of which he had come across while hunting: a story which, by the bye, may remind us of Duke William Longsword and the ruins of Jumièges.[2]

As to the date of this prologue, its lower limit is given by the fact that it was known to William of Malmesbury; and also by the mutilated condition in which it was found by the scribe of *Faustina* A 10, who, not having

---

[1] See Additional Note C.
[2] *Willelm. Gemetic.* iii. 7.

the opening words to guide him, appended it, instead of prefixing it, to his copy of the version of the Rule. The upper limit is not easy to determine. There is nothing to suggest the tenth century rather than the eleventh. The writer shows ignorance of St Ethelwold's history and of the foundation of Abingdon by K. Edred. Moreover his use of the word *canonicas* has no parallel for the tenth century. When we know more of the relation of this form of the version to other forms and to the original translation of the Rule, we may be enabled to speak more definitely as to the date. Meanwhile we must be content to refer this prologue to some unknown writer of the eleventh century.

ADDITIONAL NOTE B

ON 'WULFSTAN'S' LIFE OF ST ETHELWOLD

A FEW examples must be added to the two given above[1] to illustrate the changes made by the later writer (W.) in Ælfric's Life of St Ethelwold. I quote the pages of Mabillon's *Acta SS. Ben. Ord.* vol. vii (= Migne *P. L.* 137, 84 ff.).

P. 597. The mother of St Ethelwold requires the aid of a holy virgin to interpret her dreams. She confers with Etheldrida, 'nutrix deo devotarum virginum' at Winchester. But subsequently we are told that St Ethelwold as bishop appointed Etheldrida to be the head of the Nunnaminster—though evidently, if we trust W., she was of ripe age when he was in the womb.

P. 598. Of the coming of the soul of the child Æ. says (*Hist. Abingd.* ii, p. 256): 'sicut postea ipse sanctus qui nasciturus erat jam episcopus gaudendo nobis narravit.' W. has the same words with only the inversion 'nobis gaudendo'.

[1] p 107.

Ibid. The miracle of the removal from the house to the church is told of the saint's nurse, not of his mother: it is accordingly to the glory of the boy, and the mother's fame of sanctity is again depressed.

Ibid. At baptism the name is given as 'Adelwold' instead of 'Athelwoldus', and the spelling with 'd' is constant. Confirmation is expressly added to baptism.

P. 599. W. does not appear to understand the technical usage of Æ. (p. 256), 'ejus comitatui diu adhaerens'; and so he writes: 'ibique individuo comitatu multum temporis agens in palatio.'

Ibid. Between the tonsure and the priesthood W. inserts 'paucis labentibus annorum curriculis'. This is one of several instances of the zeal for regularity which comes out in some of the writers just after the Conquest.[1]

Ibid. 'Ædelwoldus . . . nomine, mente et opere benivolus'. Would an Anglo-Saxon have written this?

P. 600. Historical references are added from the A.-S. Chronicle.

P. 601. Æ. has 'inebriatis Northanhymbris suatim'. W. has 'inebrietate suatim Nordanhimbris'. Is this a miscopying, or does he misunderstand *suatim*?

P. 603. The Privilege of Abingdon. This seems to be a reference to the obviously forged charter, B.C.S. 1047, from *Hist. Abingd.* i. 255 ff. ('ipsius [*sc.* Edgari] privilegium').

I feel little doubt that any one who compares the two Lives, sentence by sentence, with these hints to guide him, will come to the conclusion that a Winchester monk of Bishop Walkelin's time wrote up his famous saint after the approved fashion of his day. His work is useful for textual purposes. It gives us *Wiltuniensis* (p. 601) for Bishop Ælfstan's see, instead of the corrupt *Wintoniensis*; and it tells us that Wulfstan *æt Delham* (p. 602) was the king's representative who came to drive out the clerks from the Old Minster. But its additions

---

[1] Cf. *St Oswald and the Church of Worcester*, pp. 46–8.

are of no value: e.g. its statement that Ethelwold was made *decanus* at Glastonbury (p. 600).

The expanded Life (W.) is found in *Nero* E I, f. 415 *b* (old reference): and Hardy dates this MS 'xi cent.' But whereas the greater part of this collection of Lives of the Saints is of the eleventh century, the last few Lives are in a hand of about the middle of the twelfth century, and amongst these is St Ethelwold's, the present reference to which is *Nero* E I, pt. ii, f. 209 *b*. For this information I am indebted to Mr. J. A. Herbert.

ADDITIONAL NOTE C

ON THE USE OF THE TERM 'CANONS'

WE have referred above to the change of *clerici* into *canonici* in 'Wulfstan's' enlarged recension of Ælfric's Life of St Ethelwold, and to the use of the word *canonicas* in the so-called postscript to the English version of the Rule in *Faustina* A 10. I give here such evidence as I have come across of the use of the word 'canons', with a view to justifying the statement that the term is not found, except in some foreign context, in English documents until after the tenth century.

1. An early and isolated instance is found in 787, when the Legates George and Theophylact report to Pope Adrian their proceedings in England. Among their *capitula* is one which deals with 'vita et habitus canonicorum', and begins: 'Ut episcopi diligenti cura provideant, quo omnes canonici sui canonice vivant' (Haddan and Stubbs, *Councils*, iii. 450). But this is not a document of home origin.

2. In the *Regularis Concordia* I have noted the following (the pages are those of the *Monasticon*, vol. i):—

p. xxxvi: capitula canonici cursus.

p. xxxvii : et canonico more.

p. xxxix : ac silenter more canonicorum, ut supra diximus, decantet.

p. xl : completorium sonoriter celebratur more canonicorum in die sancta Paschae . . . more canonicorum propter auctoritatem beati Gregorii papae (*et bis infra*).

Here we have simply a liturgical term. In Albers, *Consuet. Monast.* v. 41 (a Trèves MS), we read that the 'cursus canonicorum' is, as here, to be followed at Easter: cf. ibid., p. 35, 'cursum sancti Petri'. Other examples are 'cursus canonicus horarum', i. 160 ('Farfenses'); 'canonicum completorium', iv. 247, 250 (Vallembrosa); 'nocturnale officium legaliter canonicum', v. 125 (Verdun).

3. Whereas in the Parker MS of the A.-S. Chronicle (A) we read under 964: 'Her dræfde Eadgar cyng þa preostas,' we find in F, a Canterbury MS of the twelfth century 'þa canonicas', and in E (*c.* 1121) 'Hic expulsi sunt canonici'. Thus we see the term 'canons' supplanting the earlier term 'priests'.

4. In the Laws of K. Ethelred (*c.* 1008) we find the word *canonicas*. But here we have an indication that its use is somewhat a novelty. In v 7 the word appears once, and it is found likewise in the parallel recension vi 4. But it is to be noted that at an earlier point the two recensions do not thus coincide: for vi 2 has: 'bishops and abbots, monks and mynchens, canons and nuns' (canonicas 7 nunnan); but v 2 has *preostas* instead of *canonicas* : cf. 'preostas and nunnan', quoted by Liebermann from 'Hom. n. Wulfstan, ed. Napier 269'.

ADDITIONAL NOTE D

ON THE 'ALEA EVANGELII'

In order to facilitate the comparison of parallel passages in the Four Gospels, Eusebius of Caesarea divided each Gospel into sections numbered consecutively from the beginning to the end. Thus St Matthew's Gospel was numbered from 1 to 355, St Mark's from 1 to 233, and so forth. He then constructed a Table of Ten Canons. The First Canon contained the numbers of the sections which were found in all four Gospels, arranged thus—to take the first line for example:

Mt	Mc	Lc	Jo
8	2	7	10

This shows at a glance that the section about the Voice crying in the Wilderness, which is the eighth section in St Matthew, will be found as the second section in St Mark, and so on. In the margin of Mt iii 3 (to use our modern verse-division) is placed $\frac{8}{1}$, to indicate that the parallels to section 8 will be found by reference to the First Canon.

The Second Canon similarly shows the sections which are found only in Mt, Mc and Lc; and where these occur in the text of each of these Gospels the number of the section will have the figure 2 beneath it.

The contents of the Canons may be set out thus:

1. Mt Mc Lc Jo
2. Mt Mc Lc
3. Mt Lc Jo
4. Mt Mc Jo
5. Mt Lc
6. Mt Mc
7. Mt Jo
8. Lc Mc
9. Lc Jo
10. Peculiar sections.

These Eusebian Canons were, as is well known, adopted by St Jerome in his edition of the Vulgate.

At the top of f. 5 b of the Corpus MS (see the facsimile) is a group of five tables. The first table shows the canons in which Matthew occurs. It has six columns: col. 1 shows the number of the canon; col. 2 the number of Evangelists contained in that canon; cols. 3–6 the initials of the Evangelists thus contained. The next three tables are similarly arranged for Mark, Luke and John.

The fifth table shows the number of groups of parallel sections contained in each canon.   When we compare these numbers with those shown in the Table of Canons printed by Wordsworth and White for the Latin Vulgate, we find four points of difference.   For can. 1 we have 71 instead of 74; for can. 2, 109 for 111; for can. 5, 83 for 82; for can. 6, 49 for 47.   In the first three instances our numbers are borne out by (e. g.) the Book of Armagh and the Lindisfarne Gospels; in the fourth instance these codices have 48.   Thus we are obviously dealing with a variant Irish tradition.

The paragraph which follows these summary tables is confusedly written:

In his .x. sunt ordo et numerus et multiplicatio.   In uno (id est in primo canone *above line*) concordant.   In .VIII. (id est canone *above line*) vero bina. in uno alio nulla respondent. id est numerus et multiplicatio.   Ordo vero corruptus est quia lucas in tertio canone ponit (*?for* ponitur) ante marcum.

The last sentence refers to the fact that can. 3 contains Mt Lc Jo, and can. 4 Mt Mc Jo: thus Luke has precedence of Mark.   This point of order is touched on again in the explanation of the *alea*, and fanciful reasons are offered to account for it.

The next paragraph introduces the *alea* thus: [1]

Incipit Alea Evangelii, quam Dubinsi episcopus Bennchorensis detulit a rege Anglorum, id est a domu Adalstani regis Anglorum, depicta a quodam Francone et a Romano sapiente, id est Israel.

Si quis voluerit scire hanc aleam plene, illi ante omnia hujus discipline documenta hec .VII. scire animo necesse est : duces scilicet et comites, propugnatores et impugnatores, civitatem et civitatulam, et .IX. gradus bis.

---

[1] See above, p. 70.

After the great diagram there follows on f. 6 *a, b,* a full description of the *alea*:[1]

Iudeus Romanus et Franconus peritissimi .IIII. evangeliorum ut per ordinem canonum .x. multiplicationem .IIII. evangelistarum intellexerunt quadrangulam paribus figuram quatuor lateribus .x. et .VIII. tramites in longitudine et in latitudine habentem consignaverunt. Si cui autem in scropulum occurrerit quare quatuor et non tribus vel .v. hec figura lateribus conscribitur. Nec mirum est quia auctores .IIII. evangeliorum decemque canonum quatuor esse non dubium est. Hec autem quatuor est laterum et angulorum inter .IIII. evangelistas divisio. Primum quidem latus cum precedente angulo a sinistro in dexteram supra manus verticem in scribendi positione porrectum Mathei esse quis dubitat? Secundum autem latus cum antecedente angulo in quo Mathei latus finitum est . et a superiore loco dirivatum post ejusdem manus dorsum ad imum Luce esse describitur. Tertium vero latus cum angulo in quo Luce latus terminatum est subradic⟨t⟩e palme a dextera in sinistram porrectum ⟨Iohannis⟩ esse non dubitamus. Porro quartum exinde inceptum atque angulum erectum Marci esse designatum est. Tricentas vero .XXIIII. intra se habet quadrangulas ista figura. x. enim et octo octies decies in trecentos .XXIIII. consurgunt. Septem autem trianguli secundi et tertii et quarti canonis intra se haberi videntur. Porro viri qui in canonibus continentur .LXXII. esse non dubitamus. id est Matheus .xx. Marcus .xv. Lucas .XVII. Iohannes .xv. videtur. Quantumcunque enim evangelium in canonibus multiplicantur ad ampliorem numerum consurgere videntur. In canone primo Matheus quater .in secundo ter. in .III. ter . et in quarto ter . in quinto bis . in sexto bis . in . VII . bis . atque in . x . semel nominatur. Quatuor igitur semel et terni ter et bini ter atque singuli semel . XX . esse perspicuum est. Marcus vero in canone . I . quater, in secundo ter atque in . IIII . ter . in . VI . bis . bisque in . VIII . ac semel in . x . consurgere videtur. Quatuor igitur cum ⟨tribus⟩ bis

---

[1] The small letters over the figures (e.g. IIII) are not represented in what follows for typographical reasons.

ac binis bis singulisque semel . xv . virorum numerum
efficiunt. In . i . canone quater atque in secundo ter ter-
que in . iii . in . v . vero bis et in . viii . bis atque bis
in . ix . in . x . vero semel Lucas connumeratur. Quatuor
igitur cum tribus bis atque binis ter ac singulis semel ad
. xvii . summum virorum consurgunt. Iohannes porro . iiii .
in . i . canone in . iii . tribus tribusque in quarto in . vii .
duobus duobusque in . ix . vicibus atque in . x . semel connumeratur. Quatuor igitur semel atque tres bis . iique bis at
singuli semel . xv . esse non dubium est Iunge igitur . xx .
Mathei ac Marci . xv . et Luce . xvii . atque Iohannis . xv .
et . lxvii . efficiuntur. Atque his junge . iiii . varios viros qui
a Marco et ab Iohanne possidentur. Ac primarium virum
quem nullus evangelistarum possidet . et unitatem trinitatis
significantem et simul omnes lxxii ut prediximus efficiuntur.
Hi sunt viri quos varietas . x . canonum multiplicavit.
Videamus igitur quomodo isti hanc aleam possident viri.
Quadrangula quidem media . ix . quadrangulas intra se habens.
id est . v . pallidas quatuorque plenas quaternis viris primi
canonis esse videtur. Hec est autem via per quam unius-
cuiusque canonis initium reperire potueris. In quocunque
enim loco crucem cum numero reperieris initium canonis esse
non dubites. Perge igitur ad superiorem quadrangulam
magne et medie quadrangule et intra ⟨se⟩ quatuor viros
habentem id est Matheum in superiore loco et in principio
sub cruce et unario . et Lucam a sinistris Mathei. Iohannem
vero a plantis . atque Marcum a dextris possidentem. Deinde
ad aliam quadrangulam binarium supra se habentem . et
sub binario Marcum . Matheum vero a sinistris Marci ac
Iohannem a dextris . atque Lucam a plantis astantem pergere
debemus. Postea ad quadrangulam a diverso positam . et
sub ternario Lucam habentem . et a dextris ejus Matheum . et
a plantis Marcum . a sinistris vero Iohannem nunc gradiamur
Postremo ad quartam quadrangulam et sub ⟨qua⟩ternario
Iohannem et ejus a dextris Lucam . ac a sinistris Marcum .
a plantis vero Matheum habentem ingredi debemus. Eleva
nunc oculos ad Matheum in principio positum canonis secundi
ac in primo angulo ⟨trianguli⟩ et a dextris ejus Marcum ac
⟨a⟩ sinistris Lucam habentem. Ad secundum nunc triangulum

Marcum e contrario habentem . et a sinistris ejus Matheum . a dextris Lucam aspicientem pergamus. Vertamus ad dexteram et Lucam ante varium virum noscere . at post varium Marcum . ac deinde Matheum debemus. Incipit nunc tertius canon a Matheo sub cruce et ternario in primo angulo trianguli posito qui Lucam a dextris . Iohannem vero a sinistris videtur habere. Lucas quoque virginitatem et ampliorem canonis id est actuum et evangelii conscriptionem . In canonibus Marcum precedere non dubitatur. Nunc duos viros Lucam in primo ac Matheum in secundo ante varium virum loco . atque Iohannem postremo inspicere debemus. Adhuc ad dexteram vertamus . et Iohannis in . I . trianguli angulo . et Lucas ejus a sinistris . et Matheus a sinistris ejus nobis occurret. Quartus autem canon a Matheo in angulo primo trianguli sub cruce et quaternario possito incipit . qui Marcum a dextris ac Iohannem a sinistris videtur habere. Varium nunc transgrediamur virum . et postea Marcus in trianguli primo angulo . Matheum a dextris atque Iohannem a sinistris habens constare videtur . Iohannes vero in primo angulo contrarii trianguli . Marcum a sinistris . et Matheum a dextris habens non dubitamus haberi. Hic prope Matheum primarium virum habitare perspicuum est. Nunc aliam viam in reliquis canonibus inspicere debemus. Quintus enim canon et sextus . VII . atque . VIII . nonusque canon a sinistra in dexteram singuli per singulos tramites porrigi videntur. Quintum vero canonem Matheum in primo sub cruce et quinario habentem loco . Ac Matheum in fine . Lucamque bis in medio possidentem conspicimus. Senarium nunc cum cruce Matheum in principio atque in fine . Marcum vero bis in medio possidentem intueri debemus. Porro VII a septinario et cruce i⟨n⟩cipiens Iohannem bis inter duos Mathei habere nemo dubitat. Octavus quoque ab octinario et cruce incipiens Lucam primo et Marcum secundo et tertio . Lucam vero quarto loco habere videtur. Nonus vero a . IX . et cruce inchoans . Lucam in primo Iohannem vero in secundo et tertio atque Lucam in quarto loco continere perspicuum est. Decimus vero canon in quatuor locis constare videtur. Cumque enim . X . cum cruce conspexeris . X . canone deputare ne dubites. Quatuor autem varii viri qui sparsim in hac figura

conspiciuntur Marco et Iohanni deputantur. Ideo autem
varii sunt et non nigri sicut ceteri quia Marcus et Iohannes
canonem sine altera evangelista non ediderunt. Porro
primarius unum Mathei et Marci . et Luce et Iohannis .
votum vel unitatem trinitatis significare videtur. Unarius
quoque qui in medio alee perspicitur indivisibilem trinitatis
substantiam sive primi canonis principatum significat.
Quaterni quoque viri quatuor extremorum angulorum propter
alie decorem formati[1] sunt . vel ideo quia sparsim quater-
uatimque per aleam viros evangeliste possident. Unus
quisque quatuor in suo proprio angulo viros possident .
finit amen finit.

The following is a summary paraphrase of this text:

The *alea* is described as a square with 18 rows, lengthwise
and breadthwise. It has 4 sides, and not 3 or 5, because the
Evangelists are four in number. Now this is the division of
sides and angles among the Four Evangelists.

The first side with the preceding angle, reckoning from left
to right, is St Matthew's. The second side, with the angle
where St Matthew's line ends and descending from it [i. e. on
the right], is St Luke's. The third [i. e. at the bottom] is
St John's. The fourth [up the left side] is St Mark's.

324 squares are contained in the table; for $18 \times 18 = 324$.
There are 7 triangles, of the second, third and fourth canons.
72 men are contained in the canons : Mt 20, Mc 15, Lc 17,
Jo 15 [=67]. For, as the Gospels are multiplied in the
canons, they rise to a larger number:

Mt in can.	1	is named	4	times
,,	2	,,	3	,,
,,	3	,,	3	,,
,,	4	,,	3	,,
,,	5	,,	twice	
,,	6	,,	twice	
,,	7	,,	twice	
,,	10	,,	once	
			20	

[The 'four times' in which Mt is named in can. 1 may be

---

[1] Or 'firmati'. The MS has 'īmati'.

seen by the four summary tables given above, in which he appears once in each table under can. 1. The other tables are by a mistake numbered consecutively 1 to 5 (or 6) : for Jo the second line should be numbered 3 (Jo Mc Lc). If properly numbered these tables would show how the Evangelists are 'multiplied'.]

The three other Evangelists are similarly multiplied. Add then together 20 of Mt, 15 of Mc, 17 of Lc, and 15 of Jo, and they make 67. Add on the four 'variegated' men, who belong to Mc and Jo ; and the 'primary' man, who belongs to none of the Evangelists and who signifies the Unity of the Trinity : all together make up 72, as we said before. These are the men whom the variety of the ten canons has multiplied.

The middle square, which contains 9 squares—viz. 5 pale and 4 filled with groups of four men—belongs to can. 1. The beginning of each canon is to be found where there is a cross with a number.

Go to the great middle square's upper square, which has four men within it : Mt at the top, under a cross and no. 1 : Lc to Mt's left, Jo at his feet, Mc to his right.

Now go to the square with the no. 2 above it ; and under the 2 you find Mc, with Mt on his left, Jo on his right, and Lc at his feet. In the opposite square under the no. 3 you have Lc, with Mt on his right, Mc at his feet, and Jo on his left. Lastly, in the fourth square under the no. 4 you have Jo, with Lc on his right, Mc on his left, and Mt at his feet.

Raise your eyes now to Mt at the beginning of can. 2 [marked by a cross], and in the first angle [of the triangle]. He has Mc on his right and Lc on his left. Now go to the second triangle, which has Mc the other way round [i. e. in the bottom angle], with Mt on his left and Lc on his right. Turning to the right we have Lc, before we come to the variegated man, after whom we have Mc and then Mt.

Can. 3 begins with Mt under a cross with the no. 3, in the first angle of the triangle, with Lc on the right and Jo on the left. [Here we come to the problem raised above, viz. why can. 3 should have Mt Lc Jo, instead of Mt Mc Jo (which is can. 4) : why this precedence of Luke ? The answer is :]

On the ground of[1] virginity, and the larger writing of the Canon, viz. the Acts and the Gospel, Luke precedes Mark in the canons.

Next we have two men, Lc first and Mt second, before the variegated man, and lastly Jo. Then to our right we see Jo in the first angle of the triangle, with Lc on his left [? right] and Mt on his left.

Can. 4 begins with Mt in the first angle of the triangle under a cross and the no. 4, with Mc on his right and Jo on his left. [In the diagram the cross and no. 4 have been wrongly placed at the preceding triangle.]

Now we pass the variegated man, and we find Mc in the first angle of the triangle, with Mt on the right and Jo on the left. In the first angle of the triangle which is turned the other way we have Jo with Mc on the left and Mt on the right. And here next Mt is the place of the 'primary' man.

For the rest of the canons we take another route. Canons 5, 6, 7, 8 and 9 go from left to right, each on his own line.

Can. 5 has Mt in the first place under a cross and the no. 5, and Mt again at the end of the line, and Lc twice in between.

Can. 6 has Mt first under a cross and the no. 6, and again at the end, and Mc twice in between. [The second 'Mc' is missed out in the diagram].

Can. 7, beginning with a cross and the no. 7, has Jo twice between two of Mt.

Can. 8, starting from a cross and the no. 8, has Lc in the first place, Mc in the second and third, and Lc again in the fourth.

Can. 9 begins from a cross and the no. 9, and has Lc in the first place, Jo in the second and third, and Lc in the fourth.

Can. 10 is seen to stand in four places: for wherever you see no. 10 with a cross, this belongs to the 10th canon.

Now the four variegated men who are seen at separate points belong to Mc and Jo. They are variegated, and not black like the rest, because Mc and Jo put forth no canon without another Evangelist.

The 'primary' man signifies the one purpose of Mt, Mc, Lc and Jo, or the Unity of the Trinity. Moreover the figure 1

[1] *Quoque* seems a mistake for *propter*.

in the middle of the *alea* signifies the indivisible substance of the Trinity, or the supremacy (*principatus*) of the first canon.

The groups of four men at the four outer angles are there for the decoration of the playing-table ; or, since the Evangelists have men separately and in groups of four throughout the table, each one of them has four men in his own proper angle.

With this aid to interpretation we may leave the game to the ingenious reader. He will find that he can follow the setting of the pieces by a study of the facsimile. In a few instances indeed it is clear that the table has been wrongly copied. There is one man missing, as we have pointed out above; and some pieces may possibly have got on to wrong lines.

The dots placed near the men are intended to indicate the Evangelists—one for Mt, and so forth: but they do not always seem to be accurately assigned. It may be questioned whether these dots are a part of the original table, or only the insertion of some early student who was trying to identify the pieces in accordance with the terms of the explanation.

Something must be said as to the notes attached to the table itself. Some of them at any rate would seem to be independent of the formal interpretation. Thus we have in the left-hand margin a sort of reproduction of the 'variegated' man, with the statement that 'this signifies the Passion of Christ'. Again, in the upper part of the table, we have a note which is partly in Irish, and seems to mean: ' that is, resurrection or reign: for it is what Matthew tells'. In the middle of the table, near what the interpretation declares to be the place of the 'primary' man, we see the words *fer gabala* ('man of getting, invasion or conquest'). There would appear to be other Irish notes in an abbreviated form.

We may wonder whether after all this *alea Evangelii* is not rather a puzzle than a game, whether its interest does not end with the setting or identification of the pieces on the board. Yet we must remember the reference to the 'dukes and counts', and this seems to suggest that something more was intended. Otherwise the interest of this *alea* would fall short of the somewhat problematical pleasure offered by Bishop Wibold's system of dicing with the Virtues, which he invented to win the clergy of Cambrai from the gaming-tables in A.D. 965 (*Gesta pontificum Cameracensium*, Mon. Germ. Script. vii 393: Migne, *P.L.* 134, 1007 ff.; 149, 85 ff.).

INDEX

Abbo 132 f.
Abingdon, abbots of 36 ff., 39 f. ; relics at 79 f. ; revival under St Ethelwold 21, 87 f., 110 ff., 115, 160, 163 f., 168 ; privilege of 169 : *see* Chronicle, A.-S.
Abingdon, *History of* 36 f., 46 f., 72, 80, 110 f., 114, 116, 160 f., 168 f. : *see* Manuscripts
Adalbero, bp of Metz 140
Adalolf 79, 138 f.
Adamnan 56
Adrian I 170
Ælfere ealdorman 164
Ælfheah, bp of Wells 54, 82 f.
Ælfheah (the Bald), bp of Winchester 54, 82 ff., 94 f., 108, 113
Ælfheah, St, abp of Canterbury 99, 106 f.
Ælfred, bp 46
Ælfric, ab. 133, 158, 164 ; Life of St Ethelwold 105 ff., 111 ff., 160, 168 ff. ; summary of *Regularis Concordia* 105, 144, 146, 156
Ælfric, abp of Canterbury 37 f., 47 f.
Ælfsige, abp of Canterbury 113
Ælfstan, bp of Wilton 169
Ælfthryth, d. of Alfred 138
Ælfthryth, Q. 121 f., 144, 165 f.
Ælfwald, bp 59
Ælfweard churchward 79
Ælfwine, bp of Lichfield 44, 47
Ælfwyn, d. of Ethelfleda 47
Ælsi 118
Agilo 139, 141
Aidan 101 f.
Alan Twisted-beard 74, 83
Albers, Dom Bruno 150, 171
Albion 58
Alcuin 148
Aldhelm 14, 58, 69
Aldulf, abp of York 117 f.

' Alea Evangelii ' 70 f., 171 ff.
Alfred, K. 16, 36, 51, 76 f., 79, 81, 86 f., 95, 110, 138 ; work for learning and religion 13 ff., 25, 38, 41, 125, 127, 149 ; failure to revive monachism 13 f., 40 f., 142, 149 ; date of death 27, 31, 65, 82
Alfric Puer 47
Alphege, St, *see* Ælfheah, St
Amandus, St 65
Annals, Northumbrian 22, 26, 29 f., 51 f.
Annals of Ulster 56 f., 70
Anselm, St 22 f.
Aquitaine, William d. of 135
Archembold ab. 141
Armagh 59, 71
Armagh, Book of 56, 173
Arno 149
Arnulf, c. of Flanders 79, 86, 138
Arnulf, St 140
Arras MS 100
Ashdown 48
Asser 13 ff., 51, 65
Athelgeofu, d. of Alfred 14
Athelm, abp of Canterbury 15, 25, 41, 67, 82 f., 92 f., 94
Athelney 14, 81
Athelsige 37
Athelstan, ' Half-king ' 46, 49, 129
Athelstan, K. 5 f., 18 ff., 25–85, 92 f., 96 f., 108 f., 120, 127, 138 f., 173
Athelstan, priest of Worcester 13 f.
Athelwin 37
Augustine, St, of Hippo 117
Augustine, abp of Canterbury 103, 145, 160
Avranches 73

Baldwin, c. of Flanders 138
Baltonsborough 82
Bangor in Ireland 70 f., 173